KNOWN BY NAME
INSIDE THE HALLS
OF NOTRE DAME

KNOWN BY NAME
INSIDE THE HALLS
OF NOTRE DAME

James B. King, C.S.C.

KNOWN BY NAME
INSIDE THE HALLS
OF NOTRE DAME

Copyright@ 2008 by James B. King, C.S.C.

10 9 8 7 6 5 4 3 2 1

ISBN 978-0-9776458-4-8

Published by Corby Books
A Division of Corby Publishing
P.O. Box 93
Notre Dame, IN 46556
phone: 574.229-1107
fax: 574.698-7600
email: corbybooks1@aol.com

Printed in the United States of America

With gratitude to Father George who taught me to know all their names and to the Otters who have called me a few I dare not print.
Frater pro fratre!

Contents

Acknowledgments

I AM DEEPLY INDEBTED to my next door neighbor, Father Malloy, who graciously agreed to write the foreword for this book. He has been a constant support since I first came to live with a romp of frisky Otters. Barb Carlson and Ed Mack were very supportive readers of the first version of this manuscript and encouraged me to move forward. I owe a big bloody thank you to my Australian ordination classmate, Father Bill Miscamble, C.S.C., whose penetrating eye caused me about ten weeks more work but helped me to fashion a better book. It was that second draft that Matt Storin generously reviewed, and I deeply appreciate his affirmation that it merited publication.

I would also like to thank several hall clerks, Chris Hale, Pete Lavorini, and John Hennessey, who ferreted out numerous historical facts that found their way into this work. I also appreciate the kind assistance of the Notre Dame Archives staff in training them how to access the collection. In addition to those works cited within the text, I also used Notre Dame and the Klan by Todd Tucker for background material on the early days of Sorin College, Rev. Arthur Hope, C.S.C.'s timeless book, Notre Dame: One Hundred Years, and various selections from Father Moreau's writings.

A multitude of thanks goes to my publisher and editor Jim Langford at Corby Books who jumped more readily than I had imagined possible upon the opportunity to publish the first book authored by a priest whom he had never met. I am especially glad that he used a scalpel on the draft manuscript rather than a meat cleaver regardless of whatever flaws remain. I would never have made it to him in the first place were it not for the referral from Tom Grady, publisher of Ave Maria Press, who also read the second draft when I needed some extra convincing that there might be a market for it.

This book could not have been written without the material unwittingly provided by a variety of Sorin Otters. I would be remiss if I failed to specifically laud the infamous "Brew Crew" and their classmates who first entered our back doors as freshmen my first year as rector. They were indeed a most jocular bunch, and most of the characters in these pages come from their ranks. I did employ some pseudonyms to prevent embarrassment – just in case any do run for the Senate later on! I suspect those whose names I did not alter will be more red-faced by the admiration I hold for them. May the Lady on the Dome guide each of you on whatever paths you to travel after your brief sojourn in Northern Indiana.

I was immensely gratified, a little more than ten months after I wrote the first word in my journal, when Father Poorman presented Michael Dewan with the senior service award mentioned in Chapter 1. The next week he handed Pat Reidy a full-tuition Lou Holtz Scholarship for Leadership, also based largely upon his work with St. Jude's. Walking out of the office afterward, I turned to Pat and said, "I'm not sure how much you believe in the Bible, but you just got back a hundredfold what Molly handed you." The presentation of two significant University awards in successive weeks to Michael and Pat confirmed why they deserved to be the bookends of this manuscript.

Many thanks also to those who have gone to Uganda in one form or another these past several years: Steve Merjavy, Ben Wilson, Pete Quaranto, Matt Young, Kevin Bailey, Shawn Finlen, and Michael McDonald. You have made a difference in more lives than you will ever know. And my everlasting gratitude to John Fogarty, Class of '49, and his dear wife Leafy, whose generous endowment gift guarantees that an Otter can go to Uganda every summer for as long the bricks of both Sorin College and St. Jude School hold together.

A humble thank you to all those who have served on my Sorin hall staffs: LT, Dan, Stevo, Steve, Bart, Mikey, Matt, Nick, Mike, Vinnie, Alex, Dylan, Matt, Jimmy, Dan, Tony, Tony, Tim, Sush, Greg, Matt, Pat, Rob, Tyler, Phil, and John. Every year it does go as you go, and I hope you forgive this occasional ogre his sporadic, idiosyncratic outbursts. I am grateful to you as I am to all those from my parents, Sam and Betty, to the most wayward sophomore who has taught me some worthwhile lesson about fidelity or forgiveness. And, by the way, Mark, thanks for the rector job. As you predicted, it certainly did get better. Lastly, my deepest appreciation to my brothers in Holy Cross who have supported my ministry and guided my life's path these past thirty years. They taught me Father Moreau's philosophy of education by their example long before I ever read Christian Education. I know he would be pleased that they are still living it. Too many to mention, they remain collectively the Heartbeat of Notre Dame.

Foreword

FR. JIM KING AND I SHARE RESIDENCE IN SORIN HALL along with over 150 male students, including two graduate student assistant rectors and four undergraduate residence assistants. Sorin Hall is the oldest and most tradition-laden residence facility on campus. Father King became Rector in 2003 and he has provided excellent leadership for the dorm ever since. Like all Notre Dame rectors, he has had to develop a tolerance for late night hours, occasional cacophony, constant interruptions, changing fashions and peer-driven fads, and mastery of the myriad details connected with the supervision of an old building and a slew of seventeen to twenty-two year olds.

In the Notre Dame residence model with its constant evocation of notions of family and community, the rector is expected to be, among other things, a warm pastor, a trusted counselor, an effective preacher and liturgical leader (at least for the priest rectors), a fair disciplinarian, a savvy manager, and a holy model of Christian living. It is amazing really that so many devoted men and women, like Fr. Jim King, have served with such distinction. In this role which is so critically connected to the University's mission as a Catholic university.

Known by Name is an insider's view of the Notre Dame residence tradition as experienced by a Holy Cross priest absolutely devoted to the students entrusted to his care in Sorin Hall. Jim King does in fact know his charges 'by name'. He greets the first-year students and their parents at the beginning of each school year with great enthusiasm and with a realistic picture of how the parent-child separation might best proceed. From that point on, as he well describes it, the dynamics of roommate relationships, of homesickness, of academic anxiety, and of peer acceptance become the focus of the rector's role. And in the wider arena, Jim helps us understand all of the issues that arise when young men (and women) are on their own and, as a result, refining their own values, friendship patterns, and modes of living in the world.

Unlike the recent spate of participant observer books where faculty members or administrators or novelists spend brief periods of time living with undergraduate students and then report on what they learned, this book draws upon a rich reservoir of personal involvement over multiple years (including Jim's own undergraduate time at Notre Dame). It presents Sorin Hall as a kind of microcosm of student life in a Catholic university context in the mid-decade of the 2000s. The picture here is unvarnished, straightforward, and full of insightful observations about the academy and about contemporary culture. But in the end, it is a story full of hope and promise. For what greater joy can there be than to have the opportunity to help mold and inspire successive generations of bright, talented, hard-working, and generous students, who may not be perfect, but who, God-willing, will do great things with their lives.

Known by Name is a welcome addition to the growing literature on the undergraduate residential experience. It is well-written, comprehensive, and fun to read. The greatest praise I can offer is to say that the Sorin Hall that Jim King describes sounds amazingly like the one I have happily resided in for over 25 years.

REV. EDWARD A. MALLOY, C.S.C

INTRODUCTION

OUR TWO-TONE GREEN '73 PONTIAC CATALINA with the vinyl top pulled up to the Main Circle on Saturday, August 27, 1977, short five and a half gallons of regular leaded after the eighty-nine and a half mile drive from the South Side of Chicago. My only previous experience of group living was a single three-week stint at White Sox Boys' Camp on Lake Winnebago in central Wisconsin five summers before. I wouldn't be eighteen until November. Going off to Notre Dame was like jumping onto a Star Trek transporter and beaming down to an unknown planet. I was excited, scared, willing, yet woefully unprepared.

Mine was an insular world lived mostly within a ten-mile radius of St. Gabriel Parish at 45th and Lowe Avenue, a couple of blocks from the old Chicago Stockyards. I had attended St. Rita High School to the southwest, on 63rd and Claremont, for four years. Every so often, I would get on a bus and go to the Loop but rarely beyond it. By the end of my senior year of high school, I had only traveled to eight states. Thirty years later, I have seen forty-seven, all except for Maine, North Dakota, and Hawaii and traveled to twenty-four countries. I go now to the North Side of Chicago more frequently to visit friends I have made in the years since, but a feeling lingers vaguely from my childhood that I am crossing a hostile international border whenever I pass north of the Lake Street "L" tracks in the Loop.

It took some years after that first ninety-minute trip along the Indiana Toll Road to realize that I had come of age in a time warp, a one-half square mile Irish Catholic enclave that narrowly escaped becoming a victim of white flight in the 1960s. Very recently, young professionals looking for starter homes close to downtown Loop have sent 125-year-old wood-framed, two-flat home prices skyrocketing. For most of the last thirty years as the world changed dramatically around it, the neighborhood of Canaryville remained firmly in the custody of grandchildren and great-grandchildren of Irish immigrants who felt more comfortable within its confines than in trendier parts of the city or suburbs.

Beyond anything I envisioned for myself when our Pontiac stopped to unload suitcases filled with bell-bottom jeans and knee high tube socks, I have spent twenty-three years, nearly half my life, in student residence halls, including five at the University of Portland. Aside from a jail, an uninhabited Pacific atoll, and the neighborhood of my youth, there are few universes smaller than a single-sex residence hall at Notre Dame.

The entire campus is about the same size and as self-sufficient as a medieval town. We have a variety of eateries serving everything from cheeseburgers to crème brulee, a power plant, a seminary and parish, a health and counseling center, fire and police departments, our own post office, orchestras, theaters, a museum, choirs, bands, and a few athletic teams too. The experience of Notre Dame broadened my worldview considerably, but it too is a self-contained entity revolving in a different orbit from the adjacent city of South Bend.

Notre Dame, like any college or university, is a self-regenerating fountain of youth. The faces change, but the population remains ageless. The permanent residents and long-term employees feel the gap increasing every year, and it is more of a chore to surmount it. While I have become adept at altering pictures in Photoshop and generating Excel spreadsheets, my fingers flex less nimbly over X-Box controls. I have yet to invest in an iPod and have given up on following music trends. I am happily relieved that many of our students are retro enough to prefer blasting Springsteen, Foreigner, and Boston tunes from their windows on Friday afternoons than hip-hop, techno, or whatever I haven't heard of yet that is out of style before I knew it was in vogue.

I was a bit pleased with myself a couple winters ago when at forty-six I joined in on one of their snow football games. I wound up at the emergency room after an hour or so, but it was a nineteen year old's blood dripping on my front car seat from the tackle I'd earned an assist on. I should be wise enough to stay in retirement from this point onward, but I remain tempted occasionally to lead with my shoulder and send one flying into a snow bank, especially after five or six months of frustrations with their growing pains have accumulated.

I am amused each year to see freshmen emerge from minivans and SUV's shorter than our yacht-sized Catalina every August, looking like dazed sheep that have wandered into an invisible electric fence. During those first couple of weeks, freshmen are more gullible than they will ever be again before dementia claims them and will do virtually anything they are told.

I realize now that it is natural to be unprepared for college, even for those who are well-traveled prior to arriving for their first year. I have seen many who thought themselves to be world wise stumble, but fortunately there are more imaginary tragedies than real ones. At Notre Dame, they are also watched over and cared for more than they will realize until they become parents themselves. As our Vice President for Student Affairs, Rev. Mark Poorman, C.S.C., said to me a few days after the Virginia Tech shootings in April 2007, "We have many layers of protection here."

Some of the people running our residence halls have spent a decade or more as rectors and are twice as old or more as their typical counterparts elsewhere. They are often overqualified for the job description on paper. It is not unusual for rectors to tap into their own list of personal and professional contacts to boost a student's future prospects or assist their well-being. We enjoy a legendary sense of community within our walls, but knowing our students well also helps to keep them safe in a culture that is generally transient and increasingly frightening.

The overwhelming number of those who arrive glassy-eyed at seventeen or eighteen depart here four years later with noticeable improvement in their social skills and maturity levels. In many cases, they have developed better priorities, stretched their intellects, and expanded their hearts too. In between they are almost endlessly entertaining, though by the end of the academic year in May I claim to welcome the lazy months of summer gratefully. Like most other rectors on the Monday following Commencement, I exclaim, "Thank God they're gone!" Rarely do I compensate for my rashness and concede aloud forty-eight hours later that I'm a little depressed not to have one knocking on my door whenever I raise the footrest on my recliner and reach for the remote control.

First-year parents who attend my talk during Orientation Weekend hear my descriptive litany of what a rector does. I tell them:

> *They knock all day long in irregular and unpredictable intervals: for scotch tape, envelopes, paper clips, and screwdrivers, or even a needle and thread. After their underwear sits in the bathroom for a week, I just pick it up with a stick and throw it in the garbage can because the RA's (senior year resident assistants) won't touch it, and I don't want to either.*

> *I've given ironing lessons and tied bow ties. I make a five-gallon pot of chili every two weeks. If it's true that the quickest way to a soldier's heart is through his stomach, then it's certainly true of an eighteen-year-old human garbage disposal. One actually knocked on my door a couple years back and asked, "Do you know how to boil water?"*

> *I've also been asked, "Do you know any place where I can live rent-free this summer?" — in mid-May. I actually delivered on that one. I pick*

up their clothes in the hallway; I pick up their clothes in the laundry room. When I get tired of seeing their stuff, I pick it up and hide it and wait to see if they notice, which they usually don't. At the end of the year, I make St. Vincent dePaul very happy. Do you get the impression that I spend a lot of time picking up after them?

They come to me and ask me where their package from home is. This is a black shirt I'm wearing, not a brown one. Do I look like the tracking service for UPS? I've given advice on how to ask a girl out on a date, even though I'm just a little rusty. I tell them not to wear brown shoes with blue suits on a job interview, and then I suggest a haircut. Last year, I loaned out my wingtips to a senior wearing two different black shoes on his way across campus to meet with a potential employer. Sound familiar?

I go to all their interhall football games in the fall and boxing matches in the spring, and occasionally to hockey, soccer, and lacrosse games too. When I don't go to one, they come up and say, "How come you didn't come to our game tonight?" It doesn't matter if I was saying Mass or in a confessional for two hours. I'm supposed to be there because I don't have anything better to do. It's not that I'm a twenty-four-hour house servant, a nanny, or an au pair. I'm just a stay-at-home priest.

While there is a vocation shortage in the Catholic Church, a majority of rectors in charge of Notre Dame residence halls are still priests, brothers, or sisters, and most of the men's halls are staffed by members of the Congregation of Holy Cross. Despite serious personnel needs in many other places, there is not another major Catholic college or university with as large a proportion of religious men and women so deeply invested in the nitty-gritty of its students' lives. I may be biased in believing that presence is the glue which prevents more real crises from developing and makes the dorm experience so meaningful for our students. I do fear the prospect of it lessening over the next several decades as the University continues to expand at a greater rate than we can provide staffing for it.

Nevertheless, I also know that these years have indelibly shaped my own priesthood, and they have vicariously enhanced my understanding of parenthood as I have dealt with the near-grown ones deposited outside my door each year. Classes of them come and go along with faddish trends in clothes, music, and technology. If they change over time, it is mainly because of environmental and cultural shifts that engulf us all, not because being eighteen means something fundamentally different than it did one or ten generations ago. Since 9/11 and more recently the shootings at Virginia Tech, we have edged closer to an Orwellian world of constant surveillance, and I wonder whether future generations will still find the forbidding images of *Robocop* absurdly fictional. The doors to our halls used to be unlocked throughout the daytime hours; now they can only be opened by swiping an ID card. It is not so fantastic to imagine a future decade when fingerprint, voice, or corneal identification will be required for entry.

Nevertheless, I cling to hope that thirty or more years from now grandparents will still regale children with nostalgic stories of their college youth. I prefer to imagine young eyes rolling lazily as elders reminisce about Facebook and gas-guzzling SUV's, just as today's undergraduates do whenever I wax on about electric typewriters, noxious purple mimeographs, and black rotary phones. But whatever the next era's characteristics, I suspect that the basic needs of college students will remain fairly constant: to be known and cared for, listened to patiently, indulged in small things, and get taken down a few pegs when they do something stupid, even if they think they are too old to need it.

It may be trite for me to say that I could not have imagined this life. Who among us can predict as teenagers more than a sliver of our personal fate, let alone the shape of the times we will inhabit as adults? It matters less that I did not predict it and more that now, so far removed in time from my birth enclave, it is difficult to envision a more rewarding one.

*   *   *

There were still a lot of South Side Irish brats like me in the 1970s. Most of my crowd wound up as carpenters, electricians, steelworkers, or firemen. Some graduated from local colleges. We all lived within three blocks of one another, and a fair number haven't moved from the homes they were born in. I was an exception, one of the few to leave the neighborhood for college.

In The *Quiet Man,* dated now but a favorite flick growing up in a parish with an altar sporting a mosaic band of shamrocks, the John Wayne character, Sean Thornton, returns to Ireland to reclaim his native homestead. As he negotiates for the land of his birthplace, he says to its owner, the Widow Terlan, "Ever since I was a kid living near the slag heaps, my mother's told me about Inishfree and White O'Morn. Inishfree has become another word for heaven to me." The widow pithily notes that Inishfree is far from heaven, and he is soon thereafter disabused of many romantic notions about his newly adopted home.

An authentic Irishman's grandson has also grown more realistic over thirty years. It was a dream to leave behind the shadow of the Stockyards for Notre Dame. There is a touch of heaven here, but it is also dangerous to put too much faith in headlines generated by one's own public relations mill. I hope the readers of this book are satisfied by my effort to put aside most of the myths and catalog the humanity of those with wacked out hormones who roam our halls for a few short years before venturing out into a wider and less forgiving world.

My own first night on campus, I was lying alone in the bottom bunk of 145 Alumni Hall with a horrendously painful toothache after a downtown Chicago dentist crammed a crown on my front tooth too tightly the day before. I feared that I was tumbling rapidly behind in the social pecking order of my new classmates and would never catch up as I listened to them mingling outside in the hallway and greeting one another hesitantly.

By the next day, I could move around without feeling like an anvil was pounding my gums and circulate around the corridors. Most other freshmen I found came from Notre Dame strongholds and introduced themselves to me as residents of Chicago, Detroit, Minneapolis, and St. Louis, but almost universally they meant Wilmette, Grosse Pointe, Edina, or Webster Groves. Very shortly thereafter, I picked up enough visual clues to become self-conscious about my wardrobe. I gradually replaced my bell bottom jeans with Levi's 501's, button-down shirts, and fashionable Topsiders to fit in better with the prep school crowd. Nevertheless, I was also surprised and pleased when I realized that the gradually emerging social divisions had little to do with our dad's or mom's salaries.

When I think back to those days, I realize that the mistakes we made transcended categories like region, class, and religion. I hope that none of my classmates ever write a book about them, or if so, that they emulate my discretion in changing names to protect many of the guilty who have made the cut here. If I seem to dismiss many of our current students' follies too readily in these pages, it is mainly because I reluctantly remember when I was young, naïve, and even stupid on occasion too. I like to think my own fuzzy undergraduate recollections allow me to identify somewhat with the insecurities of this generation, even if their eyes do roll when I ramble on about the glory days when former Coach Ara Parseghian's football teams were criticized for going 9-0-1. I hope it is more than an illusion from a not-so-hot former jock that I still understand a few things about coming of age at Notre Dame.

While I do not want to minimize the lasting scars borne by some who get rocked after encountering the tempting freedoms of the college world, overall my life here has left more entertaining memories and unanticipated blessings. I also figure it is a sign of God's ironic sense of humor that part of my life's penance is to deal with the very sins I inflicted against an earlier generation of Holy Cross priests. I am grateful that they have been most forgiving and helpful in teaching me how to be as patient as they were now that it is my turn in the hot seat.

Thirty years later, after more time dwelling at Notre Dame than on Chicago's South Side, I can pass as a reasonably well-bred Notre Dame alumnus with only a bare hint of Mayor Daley-ish "deses, doses, and dems." I've acquired several advanced degrees and enough polish when it suits me to entertain friends and donors, though I have to gear myself up mightily for cock-tail chit-chat. I regret sometimes that I am now more familiar with the airport restaurants in Cincinnati and Atlanta than my old friends' homes.

Yet while I've wandered occasionally, I wonder if I have moved far at all in the three decades since I first stepped foot on Our Lady's campus. Despite disparities of education and income, the two worlds in which I have spent most of my life are more similar than they initially appear. The acreage of each is about the same. Both are tightly bounded, set apart from surround-ing neighborhoods by undeveloped lots, fences, roads, and gates. The neighborhood of Canaryville and the University of Notre Dame are defined by their Catholic heritages yet struggle today to retain their identities. Despite the University's founding by Frenchmen, the progeny of Irish immigrants have been central characters in its history too.

Walt Disney may have been right: no matter how far we roam, it is a small world after all. Hopefully, the tales that follow will be of some interest to those who have dwelled for a while within the friendly beige brick walls of Notre Dame that have become my home and to others who simply wonder what it is like to enjoy the privilege of living here.

CHAPTER 1

IT SHOULD BE DONE

NEW FRESHMEN PASS THE MAIN GATE halfway up Notre Dame
Avenue and wriggle around the curves of Holy Cross Drive to
their new homes by following handcrafted signs strategically
placed along the road. "Zahm – the best seven years of your
life!" may be the most humorous, even if it does nothing to set-
tle parental stomachs anxious about their child's departure from
the home nest.

Of course, I will always have the greatest sentimental attach-
ment to "Alumni Hall – Center of the Universe." Its world view
may be pre-Galilean, but those words on a banner hanging from
the residence's crenellated Gothic tower in 2007 were the very
same ones that greeted me as I first rode up to the Main Circle
listening to *Bohemian Rhapsody* on our Catalina's AM-FM radio
thirty years earlier.

My own residence, Sorin College, has an otter as its hall mascot
and is home for 151 undergraduates, two law students, one university president emeritus, and me. It is the only Notre Dame residence hall that refuses on principle to hang any welcoming signs

13

on trees, in front of rocks, or (illegally) on metal stakes along the Indiana Toll Road during Orientation Weekend at Notre Dame. The mother of all dorms simply refuses to provide roadside assistance to dazed and confused newcomers. The men of Sorin assume that even stupefied newbies and their parents should have little difficulty locating us in the southern shadow of the Basilica of the Sacred Heart, the tallest landmark hovering over campus. More importantly, they don't do road signs pridefully for the simple reason that every other hall does, and we are innately superior to them.

It is only one of the quaint, minor traditions maintained by the nation's first Catholic residence hall with private rooms. Sorin residents revel in a regal disdain for recreational activities that are standard elsewhere on campus. They even abstain from cheering at football pep rallies. A few years back, they returned en masse from one, giddy with glee. Their trademark apathy had visibly irritated a football coach who called upon them several times by name only to be met with a deafening silence, dampening what little spirit circulated around the arena during a miserably mediocre season. He did not endure beyond it, but their practiced indifference has for decades.

We used to be a hall, but some 1960s radicals decided to protest the Vietnam War by issuing a short-lived proclamation of secession from the University in 1969. The protest didn't last long, but a small wooden sign on the porch lintel, reading "Sorin College" in traditional gothic lettering, remains. Anyone who reaches the front porch will spot that sign along with more recent additions – a large blue and gold welcome mat and a glazed window above which both read "Sorin College, est. 1888."

14

Unfortunately upon arrival, new freshmen ride up the slight hill leading away from St. Mary's Lake, one of two on campus, and enter through one of the four unadorned doorways at the rear. They don't see the rug, window, or wooden plaque facing God Quad. The grassy oval surrounded by a path of gray and tan pavers gets its informal name from the confluence of Dome, Basilica, statues, and other nineteenth- century Victorian-Gothic buildings that wrap around it.

Thus, our newbies initially miss the campus' finest porch as they tumble out of vehicles crammed with clothes, posters, computers, stereos, bikes, and plastic space-saving bins. They find it soon enough, however, and can be spotted there within a few days listening to upperclassmen eager to educate them about the hall's traditions, including some which do not have my blessing.

One freshman my first year in Sorin College arrived with a perfect 1600 SAT score and forty-seven Advanced Placement credits. Test scores like that do occasionally lead me to question the need to put them through a first-day driving test to determine whether they are sharp enough to find the place. By the time an entire class drifts in with average SAT marks nearing 1400, most are certifiable overachievers, and some are downright neurotic. As our own president emeritus, Rev. Edward "Monk" Malloy, C.S.C., once noted, it is all too easy for ambitious Notre Dame students to confuse their GPA with their self-worth.

A few burn out after a year or two and plunge into a psychological freefall, wondering why they have invested so much of their lives in mastering testing material and so little asking why it was important. Most, however, continue in succeeding years to

be high performance academic machines, despite the cold water shock when they get a 'B' on a test for the first time since third grade. All but one classmate will eventually survive the realization that he or she will not reprise the high school experience of delivering the valedictory speech.

Michael was one of those students who arrived through a back door of Sorin College during my first year as rector, although he showed up with an excellent head start from the human development angle. The summer after his sophomore year, malaria struck him hard and laid him up for a week after landing in Uganda to begin an eight- week service placement. By the time he returned home in August, he had melted off almost thirty pounds he couldn't afford to lose. I don't recall meeting him when he first walked in the back door his freshmen year almost two years earlier. Fifty-two freshmen had checked in with him within a few hours on a muggy Friday, arriving sporadically like a lost and bewildered flock.

However, a few years after he first walked in through one of our rear doors, I wrote in Michael's medical school recommendation that very few students had impressed me more during these past twenty-some years. I give his genes and parents most of the credit, but a number have gotten letters nearly as strong from me. They are why I am content to be a stay-at-home priest.

*   *   *

In June 2003 I attended a PowerPoint presentation by a Holy Cross brother that showcased our community's ministries in East Africa. I had just been named the rector of Sorin College a few weeks before. I had already been informed by its inmates never to utter the words *"Sorin Hall"* unless I wanted to be forcibly returned to the sterile modernity of the newer West Quad '90s dorms that are actually south of most campus buildings. I was captivated by the slideshow and asked how we could help. He suggested a twinning relationship between Sorin College and St. Jude's, a K-7 primary school located on the outskirts of Jinja, Uganda's second largest city. At that time, St. Jude's had only one dilapidated building which would have been considered uninhabitable by Appalachian settlers in this country two centuries earlier; most classes were held outside under trees.

As football season rolled around, I discovered that we hadn't been taking up a collection at our Saturday post-game Mass, and, given my Irish Catholic background, I was dumbfounded that a Catholic institution had missed an opportunity to pass a basket in church. It was the genesis of a fundraising plan. A few months later we applied for a grant from the Holy Cross community to establish an eight-week summer position for a Sorin student at St. Jude's. We also took up a Christmas collection and applied hall fine money, levied for a variety of indiscretions, to the project. There were three applicants the first year.

A couple of weeks after Ben, our first African volunteer, got home from his summer experience, he informed me that he was collecting donations from friends and family back in Omaha to support St. Jude students. He returned to Uganda the following summer and, over the next several years, raised over $6,000 for the school.

Michael followed him the second year. Within four months of his return to the U.S., he had single-handedly raised over

$12,000, enough for St. Jude's to construct a girls' dormitory which was named after him and his family. Pat followed the third year and put together a slide show that has yielded nearly $40,000 to date. Three years and a few months later, we have surpassed $100,000 in donations to St. Jude's, mostly from the initiatives of these three students. I had never asked them to do a thing. In his medical school application essay, Michael wrote:

> *I am going to go back to Africa and I am going to invest a lot of my time, my family's time, and all of our efforts into those people. There are so many people with such great need and while I understand that a lifetime of effort could hardly put a dent in any of the poverty, I know it is for me. It is what makes me happy and I cannot wait to do it. I want to establish a primary care facility, hire national health workers, and provide affordable health services to those communities that are without. I know it should be done, and I know it can be done.*

I later copied that statement into a brochure I had printed about the school and our program. Whenever I read it, I am compelled to admit that there is something to be said for overachievers. As a graduating senior, Michael's work on behalf of Ugandan children merited him the University's highest award for community service to others beyond its walls. It was the fulfillment of the potential he exhibited several years earlier when his hall honored him as the outstanding freshman in his class. In fact, within three years, nine students from one residence hall have gone to Uganda: four summer volunteers, two for post-graduate service, two working on a research project, and one enrolled in a study abroad program.

Pete got back after spending his second semester junior year taking classes in Kampala. In the few months between the program's completion and his return to Notre Dame for his senior year, he had established a lobbying organization based in Washington, D.C., to promote the plight of the "lost children" of northern Uganda. Tens of thousands had been kidnapped and forced to kill or mutilate other kids as an initiation rite into a madman's guerilla army over two decades.

During his final year at Notre Dame, Pete was interviewed on NPR and the BBC; traveled west to make a pitch to Hollywood stars at a glittering fundraiser; was awarded a Marshall Scholarship; and received the distinguished student award from the Notre Dame Alumni Association. Coincidentally or not, a number of stories about the lost children started appearing in national news magazines about the same time, and the two sides of the conflict have since signed a fragile truce.

We like to boast about the eighty percent who do volunteer service during their time here and ten percent who spend a year or more at it after graduation. Last year my hall initiated trips during both fall and spring breaks to assist victims of Hurricane Katrina in New Orleans, and another group of sophomore Otters started an after-school project with homeless children that has expanded with a new cohort of volunteers this academic year. Not all become Tom Dooleys, but enough yearn to be Good Samaritans that I know there is a place in the American academy for a university that isn't afraid to preach the Gospel along with teaching Management. We struggle constantly to harmonize the tension created by the twin pursuits of religious virtue and academic success, but while trolling for research dollars may make us a great institution, living the Beatitudes will make us better people.

Tourists, subway alumni, and sportswriters who blow quickly through campus periodically are largely indifferent to our daily struggles and think that Notre Dame is driven wholly by an insatiable, vicarious lust for football glory. The games, ritualistic pageantry of Saturday afternoons, and the follow-up sports news chatter certainly do overwhelm our collective consciousness on twelve fall weekends; however, it's what happens the other days between games and after bowl bids are announced in early December that preoccupies those of us who endure the long Indiana winters and gusty spring days until Commencement.

The recently beatified founder of the Congregation of Holy Cross was fond of asserting the importance of enlightening the whole person in both mind and heart, in and out of the classroom. Blessed Basil Moreau, C.S.C. insisted in an unfinished treatise entitled *Christian Education* that it was a teacher's responsibility not just to produce scholars but Christians. Though he left France to inspect the community's progress at Notre Dame only once 150 years ago, he would be gratified that his philosophy of education has remained the foundation for what is often termed the "Notre Dame mystique." For most undergraduates who spend four, though seldom seven years of their lives here, what they learn about themselves outside the stadium is the heart of the entire matter.

It Should Be Done

* * * *

On a late May Sunday in 2006, I was sitting in O'Hare Airport waiting for a flight to Ireland and rereading *To Kill a Mockingbird*. Its distinguished author, Harper Lee, had received an honorary degree at our Commencement a week earlier, and the University had distributed a couple thousand free copies. After finishing, I sat pondering the character of Atticus Finch, the novel's courageous lawyer and wise father.

Some of Atticus' neighbors were appalled at how he let his children, Jem and Scout, run just a little wild, but he understood that it's alright to be a kid and act like one. They need to be given enough rope to learn from their mistakes if they are ever going to become adults, and the best parents cultivate the skill of becoming relentlessly patient. So too should rectors who coexist with college students banging daily on drum sets above their living rooms. Father Moreau went so far as to claim that patience was "the only thing that permits a teacher to rise above the difficulties inherent in educating youth."

I am grateful, however, that I was never compelled to navigate the shallow cyber world of Facebook or MySpace. I do not envy people inclined to make temporary friends on the Internet at the expense of more lasting bonds in parishes, city neighborhoods, or rural towns. Today's college students are conditioned to be geographically mobile and cynical toward institutions I revered as a child. They have witnessed enough hypocrisy in public figures and betrayal within families that they distrust any commitment which does not include an exit strategy. Many of them have already traveled to more sectors of the globe than I ever imagined, but they are far more fearful about forging lasting connections or lingering in any one spot for long.

It is true that alcohol abuse remains the most proximate cause of behavioral problems. By the time they hit junior year, most students understand their limits better than when they arrived and have a reasonable handle on it, but in the interim enough become different, less genuine people when they imbibe that discipline is primarily a matter of dealing with underage drunks. However, those of us who are currently rectors, health professionals, and academic counselors also find ourselves treating more complicated diseases of both mind and heart. Too many in this generation have expended such an inordinate amount of energy building impressive resumes as adolescents – or playing the role of adults within their own households – that they respond to those stresses by behaving more erratically once they arrive at our Main Gate. They conform to external standards of success but, robbed prematurely of their legitimate childhood, respond by devastating themselves physically and emotionally.

The social and emotional pressures imposed upon eighteen-year-old freshmen have increased dramatically, and, consequently, the bell curve of our student population has flattened over the last thirty years. At one end, we have more idealistic, well-grounded, churchgoing, certifiable poster boys and girls who emerge from the morass surrounding them more mature and selflessly dedicated to transforming some corner of the world.

At the same time, we are closing in on a thousand visits a year

22

to the campus counseling center. The other tail of the curve is mutilating themselves with razor blades, contracting venereal diseases, and seeking temporary tranquility from their insecurities through prescription narcotics in addition to rampant drinking. They are afraid to go to sleep at night for fear they might miss something entertaining that flits across a computer screen, yet they sleepwalk exhaustedly through the day, alternating between binging on studies during the week and boozing on weekends. The good news is that while the client count is climbing, there is far less stigma today to seeking professional help when needed.

Still, at that age, they retain large reservoirs of resiliency and can generally overindulge on multiple fronts for a while before heading over the brink. If anything, our students are too bright for their own good. They learn quickly how to cut corners and discriminate between the material they must absorb for a test and should scour anyway for their own enlightenment. The University's graduation rate hovers steadily around ninety-five percent, so despite the inevitable growing pains and longer-term impact of more complex traumas, only a few step on career-ending landmines during their brief years here.

The campus has grown, and the mix of issues has changed. Nevertheless, Notre Dame doggedly remains, like my original home, something of a time warp, an unrepresentative sample of the elite college population, where students hold values that differentiate them from their peers. It is surprising to outsiders that our student body remains eighty-four percent Catholic. They are typically less catechized in the faith than my classmates were, more skeptical of its authority figures, and more likely to cherry pick which doctrines they will accept. However, they are clearly more religious in motivation and practice than the mean eighteen year old with even higher average SAT scores at Stanford or Duke.

They have chosen to come to enroll at a place where Catholic symbols abound and church attendance far exceeds the norm. An intelligent young man or woman can hardly fail to perceive the differences between our admissions literature and the brochures mailed by comparable institutions. As one of my graduating seniors noted last year, "Notre Dame is a self-fulfilling sociological phenomenon." More may matriculate here because of our top twenty ranking in *U.S. News and World Report* than in earlier days when we languished hopelessly far behind the elites. Nevertheless, based upon Mass crowds and volunteer program numbers, a majority appear to accept the basic proposition that faith and service are an important component of their Notre Dame experience.

We are compelled to make adjustments to new forms of personal fragility and a technologically-dependent world, yet still obliged to provide them with a safe place to work out their problems, explore their dreams, and even run a little wild at times. They have not quite finished with their Jem and Scout years, and they are entitled to enjoy the last vestiges of a carefree adolescence even as we call them to grow beyond it. Though the challenges of caring for them have grown more complex, it is hard to imagine finding as many good ones anywhere else – or as many people of any age who are as much fun to be with day in and day out.

Pondering these dynamics in a deserted section of O'Hare's Terminal 3, it dawned upon me a couple of decades living among them, riding along on the rollercoaster of their dreams and disappointments, had given me a trove of good material, even if a fair proportion of their language would need to be severely edited for a priest's book. In fact, after I returned home from Ireland, I discovered two earlier outlines covering this ground I had not mustered the will to complete.

I would like to think the students I've known have helped me to become a slightly better man and priest too. I realized what I should do is write about them and attempt to capture something about daily life in Notre Dame's residence halls, so I started taking notes in the black Moleskine journal that I had fortuitously packed. Nevertheless, as I boarded the plane I wondered whether Michael would overachieve once again at Yale Medical School and return to Africa, driven by his ultimate ambition of opening medical clinics numerous as McDonalds across the American heartland before I would polish off a book-length manuscript.

CHAPTER 2

SMALL FISH IN BIG

ON A WEDNESDAY MORNING in late August, prior to the arrival of our hall orientation crew, a pervasive quietness engulfs God Quad. The flowers lining its walkways make the campus look like a conservatory. In the hazy stillness of morning, the Golden Dome floats above campus. New arrivals assigned to Sorin College will shortly start turning under the arched tree canopy lining Notre Dame Avenue and aim straight for the collection of nineteenth-century brick buildings fashioned from lake marl that form the campus' heart.

Room floor tiles have been waxed and industrial strength carpets cleaned by middle-aged men and women in cotton-blue shirts struggling to ready the halls for new arrivals once summer school students and conference groups pull out. No sweaty football jerseys, hockey pads, or laundry heaps litter the corridors. The first contrast a discerning visitor notices during the academic year when entering both women's and men's halls is that one smells like a moldy locker room and the other like the perfume counter at Macy's. It will be Christmas break before campus is so calm and the hall's surfaces once again so pristine.

At that moment, I bewail the fact that everything has been put in good order only to be ruined by incoming hordes of young male barbarians who will soon have clothes piles on their floors the size of small Egyptian pyramids. But those thoughts pass quickly as the chaos of new arrivals soon overwhelms us and turns our thoughts to passing out keys and placing work orders for broken desk drawers missed on room inspections two weeks earlier. I always reassure parents that repairs will be done by Monday, knowing they'll be gone by then and their progeny could care less, preoccupied as they are with more pressing worries about how they will fit in, if they are anything like I was.

By Friday night, all the freshmen on my list have shown up, met at the back door by our welcoming crew. The veterans (mostly sophomores) spend most of that weekend lounging around the rear of the dorm in lawn chairs when they're not throwing Frisbees. It's not heavy duty, and in some cases, they sign up mainly to get back a few days early having tired of mowing lawns, taking out garbage, and trying to sneak by sleepless parents at 3:00 AM. Rectors appear less unreasonable after a summer with the folks at home.

But when those vehicles stop at the back entrance, crew members dote on freshmen they have just met like four year olds greeting the newborn come home from the hospital. Every box, bedspread, suitcase, trunk, and poster is snatched up by a crew member and carted up the stairs before either the new guy with peach fuzz who could pass for fourteen or his parents can object. Occasionally, like airport baggage handlers, they get the destination wrong, and I wind up lugging a wayward fifty-pound box up from the basement to the third floor where it belongs. Then they go back to lounging, occasionally dropping hints that I should order pizza to compensate them for working overtime. Once unloaded, the momentous roommate meeting follows.

"Hi, you're Jacob?"

"Yeah."

"I'm Brendan." They shake hands loosely. Definitely no hugs, at least yet.

"Yeah."

"How's it going?"

"Great."

Nervous, their conversational potential exhausted, the new roomies turn to look at hovering parents, who are forcing smiles and warily sizing up the new family. In my mind, it's like having the folks in the back seat of the car on the way to the senior prom. It used to be that parental units were shocked and grieved to see their son's glare silently signaling, "Leave the checkbook. Get back in the car and turn around. You've served your purpose as pack mules. Now scram!" However, there are more freshmen eyes these days imploring, "Don't leave me here alone. I've never had to share a room with someone else before. You're the security blanket I'm used to calling on my cell phone five times a day." I have grown cautious about making assumptions or even using the words "mother" or "father." Some have no relationship with a parent while others are tangled up with negotiating multiple sets.

It is certainly true that fewer act independently of whoever's house they just left now that the phrase "helicopter parent" has entered the college lexicon. My friends and I called our parents no more than once a week, unless we were really short on cash, and told them as little as possible. It is jarring now to see how many eighteen year olds crave their parents' advice and constant attention – and how many folks need our reassurances that their son or daughter won't crash-land before the end of the first week.

A few years back an e-mail message popped up on my screen from a worried mom who wrote shortly after returning home on Orientation Sunday asking me to check on her son. She had a hard time letting go and was concerned about him adapting because he was very close to his sibling brothers and quite shy. I received additional messages weekly and dutifully stopped by his room each time without letting on that she was writing me. Six weeks later I heard that he had been spotted at an off-campus party kissing a girl on the back porch in front of a hundred people. I didn't worry about him being shy anymore. I cut back on the visits to his room though I never uttered a word to Mom. The following July I was surprised to open a one-line e-mail from her with the single line: "I've had enough. You can have him back."

While most eventually get to that point, it takes a while that first weekend to clear the hallways of nervous parents and caregivers. Eventually, however, they do drive off so Jacob and Brendan can have those first few uninterrupted chats about what they want after receiving numerous, and often contradictory, decorating tips from both sets. They talk about furniture placement, not because they care about décor, but the discussion satisfies the male's need to define his turf within a room the size of a closet at home. While it may be their first ever look at bunk beds, they survive the awkward first night in a summer camp spirit before the start of classes. Their first days together do remind me a bit of White Sox Boys' Camp, but it isn't long before the atmosphere of a temporary vacation idyll dissipates.

By the time I rolled up to the Main Circle for my sophomore year in 1978, I had completed my transformation into an eternally loyal Alumni Dawg, convinced that Galileo's vision of the cosmos was deeply flawed. I also knew a new rector had been appointed. Brother John, in charge our freshman year, had decided to leave the Center of the Universe for our Holy Cross missions in Peru.

Whatever the difficulties in dealing with a more troubled population today, the late 1970s was no picnic for rectors either. The draft protests and campus riots of the '60s may have ended, but the aftermath was a lingering decade of gratuitous indulgence in drugs and alcohol within residence halls that frequently raged out of control. It wasn't a stretch to think Brother John had been so desperate to ditch us that living next to a Third World garbage heap looked like a better gig. I strolled down the hall to check in.

Rev. George Rozum, C.S.C. was sitting at a card table just behind his door. When I walked in, he stood up, stuck out his hand, and said, "Hello Jim, I'm so pleased to meet you." I was ticked. I figured if I played my cards right, I could avoid having the new guy figure out who I was for at least a month.

When my first group of freshmen walked through the back

doors of Sorin College to meet their rector their first weekend, a table was set up in front of my door, and I managed in many cases to stand up and say, "Hi Chris, I'm really glad to meet you. Welcome to Sorin College." I have been taught by Father George and a generation of Holy Cross rectors since to memorize names and faces from pictures the freshmen send in July.

It is a Notre Dame rector's very first responsibility to know his or her students by name. I've had a few tell me much later they were impressed and others report that they were freaked when I greeted them by name upon arrival. Of course, I've blown a few too. My third year in Sorin I was mortified to mix up the only two new black guys, though a bit less so when I discovered later that other Otters had done the same. In fairness, some, regardless of color, little resemble the person in the pictures, preening in prom tuxedos or letter jackets while leaning against a backyard tree. I do enjoy posting those in a glass case near the front door and listening to the upperclassmen hoot. After the first weekend, I rarely see a letter jacket again.

It was a hectic Friday that first year, so on Saturday afternoon, I was kicking back in my recliner during the few hours that weekend when just about everyone else was occupied by scheduled orientation activities elsewhere. Shortly before two o'clock I was interrupted by the phone ringing. It was a security office dispatcher telling me that the grandmother of one of those freshmen had died. She asked me to break the news to the family. Tony's parents had driven him out the day before from Massachusetts. They turned right around and headed home after deciding that he should stay here rather than return for the funeral.

The poor guy had just arrived, knew no one, and had drawn the worst assignment in the dorm, room 001. It was informally nicknamed the "Ass Palace" long before my arrival because the only reasonable way the furniture can be arranged in this triple is to stack all three beds so the top bunk rests about fifteen inches from the ceiling. In winter after the heat is turned on, the top bunky can warm his toes on the partially insulated pipes carrying scalding water across the ceiling

The walls are separating from the tiled floor which slopes about three and a half inches from the doorway to the far end of the room. There is so little space they have to open their wardrobe doors while standing to the side, then slide back in, sit on the bottom bunk, and get their legs out of the way to pull out the sock drawer. Like other basement rooms in the southern wing, these palatial quarters are shaded by a thick row of trees that get about ten minutes of sunlight per day in July.

A bear would be comfortable hibernating in there except that the room is right underneath the Quint, formerly a five but now a seven-man suite, with a turret room that is the biggest private social space on campus. For years prior to my arrival they had loyally defended one of those Sorin College "traditions" which I greeted with less sympathy. They were fond of dropping tables, cases of beer, bowling balls, or sometimes simply body slamming one another on the floor at three or four in the morning to harass the freshmen down below. I've made some pay dearly for their revelry in my efforts to stamp it out, but they can be persistent in holding onto their treasured customs. I'm eagerly anticipating the day when a 310-pound football player who needs to wake up for 6:00 AM weightlifting sessions is randomly assigned there.

Every year during orientation, I forbid the upperclassmen from referring to the room as the Ass Palace until after the parents leave. I make sure to spend some time with the ones who draw that room when they first walk in, like a doctor ushering a shaken family into the cardiac care unit after their dad's first heart attack. To lesson the shock, I smile and enthusiastically spin room 001 as an honor. "It's the first room in the nation's first Catholic residence hall," I cheerfully tell parents who realize they are going to have to cart home half the stuff their son had packed.

I also try to recruit someone who lived in it before to stand there with me and verify how much they loved it. I have no reservations about bribing students with pizza in exchange for lying on demand to parents trembling with separation anxiety. Tony and his folks had gotten the spin, but I wasn't sure he was over the room when he got hit with the grim news about his grandma's death.

Whenever something bad happens at Notre Dame, the reflexive reaction is to schedule a Mass, so I circulated word on Sunday that we would celebrate one for her the next night. At the time, maybe ten people other than hall staff knew Tony by name. I was hoping we'd get twelve to fifteen freshmen. Fifty-four students from all classes showed up on Monday night at

10:00 PM. We rarely take up a collection at student Masses, but I *always* count to see how many show up.

About a year and a half later, Tony told a group of Otters on a weekend hall retreat that watching those students walk through the chapel door was his most significant moment at Notre Dame. I knew then that he would be an RA, and so did virtually all his peers. Neither was anyone surprised when nearly four years after arriving for his first weekend he received Sorin College's highest award given annually to a graduating senior. The crowd snorted when I complimented him at the presentation by saying, "If he weren't going into teaching, he'd make a great mom." They too had seen Tony grow into one of those Christians who had invested his talents wisely and given back even more. Now that he has graduated from his RA duties in our basement watching over Palace residents and other freshmen to teach sixth graders, I will probably see him mostly on football weekends when he returns to visit.

However, like most Notre Dame alumni, Tony will be coming back regardless of the team's current record because of the lifelong friends he made during his first weekend in his new home. His first impulse was to turn away before unpacking his boxes that first weekend and return to Massachusetts with his folks for the funeral. After that Monday night Tony learned an important lesson that some people with an interest in Notre Dame never do: whether or not we beat USC is important, but over the long haul, faith, friendship, and being cared for by name matter more to those who have lived here.

*   *   *

Despite Notre Dame's $5 billion-plus endowment, the Palace is one of many rooms, particularly in older halls, that could pass for mildewed, cold-water, Hell's Kitchen walkup tenements at the turn of the last century. They are character-laden repositories of tradition, and that is the most sacred secular word at Notre Dame. Most students actually prefer these dorms to the newer cinderblock versions with air conditioning.

It helps that about twenty-three percent of our student body are alumni children and have been forewarned about what to expect. My classmates and I walked into forced doubles with surplus World War II metal lockers and mattresses mottled with sweat stains. My mother just laughed. Then again, she was the postwar, pre-cell phone generation, not the age of amenities. Every year before the freshmen arrive, I sweat about a mom or dad going ballistic with the, "I'm paying $9,000 a year in room and board for this!" speech. While I have witnessed some stunned looks, my ears have yet to be assaulted by a violent rant.

After one day here, most new freshmen have already been indoctrinated to touch the shiny toe of the three-foot founder's statue in the front hallway every time they pass. That's one way to verify that he hasn't been hijacked. In the 1950s it disappeared and for years afterward, University officials received periodic ransom notes with pictures of Father Sorin resting in front of various world wonders like the Eiffel Tower and Great Wall.

It is a committed thief who will pay extra shipping charges for lugging a miniature priest around the globe in his suitcase. The TSA might prevent Father Sorin from skipping through airports so easily these days, but now he is safely anchored into our floor with a core of concrete and rebar that only an earthquake could topple.

After a few more days, the initial shock has worn off, and I hear snatches of cell phone conversations with friends back home: "You wouldn't believe this dorm. It's great. It's like, just all this history, and the guys are really cool here . . ." After all the nervous tension associated with the herd's arrival, I am invariably relieved. My favorite rooms are the freshman quads: four guys, one large room. In four years, I've only had one freshman threaten to slit his roommate's throat in the middle of the night. Quads are an interesting social experiment that would be good preparation for a shot on Survivor.

My freshman roommate, like Tony, was from western Massachusetts. Luckily, I was assigned to a double, but as an only kid, one roommate was enough of an adjustment. I was a poli sci major; he was an engineer. I arrived with my South Side Irish accent sounding much more like Mayor Daley than I do now: "'Da Cubs haven't got a prayer to beat 'dose Mets 'dis year." John spoke like he'd taken elocution lessons from the Kennedy sisters. He did advanced calculus problems for fun and wasn't interested in baseball. I was on my high school traveling bowling team; I think he lettered in debate. He gargled for ten minutes every morning; I used toothpaste to hide nail holes in the walls at the end of the year so we wouldn't be fined. I realized he was a much better guy than I'd given him credit for, but it took a couple of years. I regret that I never told him and have lost track of him since.

One of those freshman quads from a couple of years ago specialized in blowing a plastic horn that sounded like the bleating of a pregnant moose out the window for hours at a time. One Saturday they started at 12:45 in the afternoon and went on more or less continuously until 2:00 AM. I know that I have adapted to the environment when a noise drives other students nutty without fazing me. Slamming doors, stereos with pulsating basses shaking walls two floors below, and bouncing basketballs echoing up and down the hallway rarely cause my eye to flicker. Pseudo nature calls, however, test students' patience. The horn disappeared early in their sophomore year. Not surprisingly, they managed to find other amusements since just about anything will bore them with enough repetition.

Real animal sounds occasionally emanate from residence rooms too. Perhaps when a rector appeared at dinner several years ago and told us that some of his, driving back through the countryside around 2:00 AM had climbed a barbed-wire fence, stolen a sheep, and snuck it up to their room, perhaps we should have been outraged and sympathetic. Instead, a table of priests just howled even louder as he related how the sheep went into shock and evacuated a Toro bag full of half-digested grass onto the carpet. We are accustomed to scolding them to their faces while laughing later among ourselves at their escapades. It's a coping mechanism. After twenty years, plastic horns are a most minor nuisance, at least before 2: AM.

*   *   *

A few hours before breaking the news to Tony and his parents, I had given my opening talk to the freshmen. I told them, as I have every year since, that they have gone from being big fish in small ponds to small fish in big ponds. Like a baseball player making the jump from Triple A to the majors, their academic performance is likely to suffer for a while as they make the adjustment. "It's college now, not high school; it's supposed to be hard," I say. "Don't panic if you end the semester with a 2.9," although with grade inflation most eventually do far better. While the valedictorian opportunities may be limited, getting admitted to Notre Dame is much harder than enduring to Commencement. It's simply more work to flunk out than to make the dean's list once they have surmounted the first semester's hurdles.

Aside from death and divorce, the three toughest transitions are moving, changing jobs, and marriage. A college freshman is certainly moving, and a new school is fairly equivalent to a job switch. Meeting the roommate may not rate with the wedding day, but, for an eighteen year old, it can be more traumatic than mating for life, if briefer in duration. It is not surprising to see them stumble initially out of the starting gate, especially those, who despite our best efforts to keep them busy with ice cream socials, navigate their way to off-campus parties the very first weekend.

I do give them one piece of paper that I hope makes a small dent in their psyches. It's called "Twelve Tips for a Successful Freshman Year" and is based upon a version Monk distributed in the 1980s. It used to be "Ten Commandments . . ." but in my first year, I encountered a few issues Moses didn't anticipate:

1.   Don't lie, cheat, or steal.
2.   Don't confuse your self-worth with your GPA.

3. Don't eat alone or let anyone else do so.
4. Don't do anything you wouldn't want your eighteen-year-old son or daughter to find out about later.
5. Listen to your RA.
6. Don't be afraid to ask for help.
7. Make your own choices.
8. Make it a point to learn all your classmates' names.
9. Pray regularly.
10. Remember your body is God's temple.
11. Respect other people and their property.
12. Make good friends and they'll make you a better man.

I added numbers 4 and 10 because most bad things that happen to students, whether car accidents, hospital runs, or traumatic hookups (a term with wide-ranging meaning) are almost always alcohol-fueled. If everyone did pay close attention to these line-items, most rectors and parents would sleep a lot easier at night. Of course, there are a small handful who get into trouble while sober, which is a particularly embarrassing blow to the eighteen-year-old ego.

And there are those relative few who just don't make it. I arrived back in Alumni Hall from class one afternoon my own senior year to hear that a guy down the hallway had been carted off in a strait jacket. He kept to himself a lot, but he wasn't an outcast either. There was no hint of a serious problem, but that day he had taken his entire vinyl record collection and a pile of his roommate's clothes and tossed it all out the third floor window. Then he ran across campus, stripping off his own garments one item at a time. We never saw him again.

I'd never heard the term bipolar before, though I have encountered it several times since. I was sitting in my room one night my second year in charge of a hall when a student entered my room and began to spew out apocalyptic visions featuring himself as the central messiah figure in a stream of consciousness narrative. By then, I'd had the training to understand what was happening. It took considerable effort to put him at ease and convince him to sit down with an RA in another room long enough for me to get to a phone and call security for assistance in transporting him to the psych ward of a local hospital.

I was upset that his parents had not alerted me to his condition until their phone calls had gone unanswered for three days. Now after loosening them up with a stay-at-home priest's job description and getting some laughs, I implore those who have good reason to worry to inform me if there are any preexisting conditions of which I should be aware. My junior with visions eventually graduated, but every bipolar episode increases the odds that one will never be quite right as an adult.

I have seen enough students subsequently freak out, flunk out, and drift away that my first standard for success is to get through the year without anyone dying and my second not to lose one for academic, medical, or other personal reasons. It may sound like minimal criteria, but rarely does a rector make the second. The involuntary departures may represent only a tiny proportion of Notre Dame's student population, maybe one or two people a year in any one hall, but a rector can spend many hours retroactively replaying what he or she might have done differently to prevent them.

Personally, I have been fortunate. No one under my roof has been killed, ended up paralyzed, or taken his own life while I was watching over them, though several have died later. Last year I did attend a funeral for a young alum killed in a freak motorcycle accident, hit by an inexperienced teenage driver who didn't see him. I greeted him walking into the Basilica on his wedding day just a few years after graduation, then watched his body wheeled out the same doors by his friends a year later. He is buried right next to the wrought iron fence by our main gate. I will never be able to pass through it again without saying a prayer for him though I fervently wish I didn't have to.

Wealth, opportunity, and the privileges associated with a top-flight education are a head start but no guarantee that all will be well even in the protective bubble that is Notre Dame. There are demons lurking in the pond, and while we try to remain vigilant, they are too old to be held to a curfew and don't have the rap sheets to warrant electronic ankle bracelets. Naturally, because it is their wont at that age, they often resist our efforts, and over some horrors we have no power. Usually, the damage is passing – a night in the hospital, the fright of a mugging, a minor accident that causes broken bones but does not rip apart families – but every year there is something more devastating wrought upon those who think themselves invulnerable to lousy genes, random fate, asinine peer pressure, or incredibly bad judgment.

Stitches, pools of blood, and arm bones breaking through the skin I can handle, but on weekend nights flitting wisps of paranoia lurk at the back of my mind that I'll get a phone call from the morgue after turning off the '70s best pop songs promos at 3:00 AM and heading to bed. Maybe I'm just Irish that way — or know that anything can happen to even a sensible one in the wrong place on a bad night. Thankfully, however, most of their foibles result only in hard lessons valued more as years pass or simply make for good stories right away.

CHAPTER 3

THE MELTING POT

"Time has written romance on these walls,
and here tradition finds a fitting home."
– 1925 DOME

BY **1925,** Sorin Hall had almost been around long enough to justify that reference to it in the University yearbook. It had been dedicated during celebrations honoring the fiftieth ordination anniversary of the University's founder, Rev. Edward Sorin, C.S.C., in May 1888. Other residence halls had sprung up since then: Badin across the lawn in 1897, Walsh next door in 1905, and Corby for several decades until reclaimed by Holy Cross as a residence for priests and brothers.

Morrissey, Lyons, and Howard Halls were almost ready for occupancy as part of the mid-1920s and early '30s building boom that would double Notre Dame's size. On the eve of the Great Depression, the University was an ambitious college determined to enhance its academic reputation. It had been propelled further along the road to glory when Grantland Rice wrote a sublime newspaper lead, beginning with a description of the blue-gray October sky characteristic of Northern Indiana in autumn.

Sports journalism's most famous column recounting the 1924 victory over Army forever cloaked Rice's Four Horsemen – Stuhldreher, Layden, Miller, and Crowley – in an aura of legend. Not so well known is that all four of those Horsemen spent at least one year living in Sorin before leaving the Hoosier state with their senior yearbooks packed inside their steamer trunks. Time and the yearbook's student editors were fortunate at the end of the 1924-25 academic year to have received some tips in the romantic writing department from a professional sportswriter earlier that fall.

Despite the debut of fancier new quarters on the South Quad shortly thereafter, a tradition would endure through the 1960s of reserving room 011, the southeast turret in the basement or "Sorin Sub," for football captains. Also, until the early '60s students had to be in their rooms with lights out by 11:00 PM, and the Sub rooms, despite their low ceilings and steam pipes, were desirable quarters for those with late-night plans seeking an easy means of egress.

Many other famous gridiron legends have lived in Sorin. From the evidence in fragmentary records, George Gipp apparently didn't, though the priest who came to his deathbed, Rev. Pat Haggerty, C.S.C., did. Knute Rockne and Gus Dorais, his co-conspirator in befuddling an earlier Army team with the revolutionary forward pass, are hall alums. The giants' off-field antics were also notable within the smaller universe of Sorin.

Supposedly, they were much admired for ingeniously augmenting their income by bilking the gullible and desperate in creative, if fraudulent, schemes. One story is that they masqueraded as maintenance men and walked around neighboring Walsh Hall the first week of class charging freshmen five dollars for "radiator rent": no cash, no heat come November. Other reports have them charging students sneaking back in after 11 PM curfews through their windows. Athletes and non-athletes lived together then and still do. Every year that I've lived in Sorin at least one football player has enjoyed the privilege of residing among its steam pipes in rooms the Rock would immediately recognize.

Drifting beyond the florid prose of yearbooks from that decade, the historically curious will also note row upon row of relatively homogeneous photos of students with white faces. Those of that era paging through the Dome were probably pleased at the alphabet soup emerging from the melting pot. It was not very diverse by modern standards, but that was an age when Italians and Poles living a block apart went to separate Catholic churches and belonged to warring gangs. They were largely ignorant of their complicity in maintaining more insidious racial barriers that would become the task of their children and grandchildren and great-grandchildren to obliterate definitively.

Today, Notre Dame has a minority population of twenty-three percent though its Catholic character and Indiana location have not helped it make significant strides in attracting more African-Americans. I'm not sure what the Rock would have thought about the Latino Institute or Gender Relations Center because he was from an era when people sought to obscure their roots and differences in order to fit in, but he sure would have loved the new $22 million football complex.

The lion's share of Notre Dame students today are very upper middle-class, though like college students virtually everywhere in the U.S., you would not know it from their standard uniform of baggy shorts (even in winter), t-shirts, and flip-flops. Of course, the young have a high tendency to conform in every era. A hall picture from the turn of the century that hangs in the Sorin College entryway depicts twenty-three residents decked out uniformly in suits, although a good many of them appear hung over from the night before. In that respect, there has been little change in a century.

It is oddly comforting that students drank excessively even when governed by draconian rules that could lead quickly to suspension. At some point, it is simply in the genetic code of most young adults to test those limits whatever the era, no matter how expertly we mix cocktails of rules, punishments, counseling referrals, and threats. Colleges and universities may get sued more readily these days for the resulting accidents and hospitalizations, but their moral culpability has its limits even as their legal liability has expanded dramatically.

*   *   *

The fourth- or fifth-generation descendants of European immigrants are much more affluent than their forebears, though substantial additions to our financial aid budget have alleviated some worries that we are becoming a rich kids' school. Fortunately, Notre Dame remains a place where students rarely brag about family wealth, though one can often infer it from their vacation stories or visits to their homes. The white collars far outnumber the blue, but the offspring of steamfitters room easily with CEO's sons. One of the most popular Sorin Otters is an unpretentious, if slightly quirky, 5'2" farm boy squirt nicknamed "Biggie," hailing from a dusty podunk in the heart of Kansas. The quickest way to become a pariah in Sorin or any other hall isn't to be a bookworm but a snotty rich kid flaunting his checkbook, even if those offended are busily gearing up for entry level salaries of $80,000 of their own at Morgan Stanley. Whatever diversity issues we may have, class warfare is not part of the dynamic.

I was reading an application statement once from an RA in which he recounted a conversation with a professor teaching in the University's London Program. He asked for the prof's opinion about how Notre Dame students are perceived beyond our walls. The latter replied that they were "real good, friendly people," and that they were generally more successful than their peers in the so-called "real world" because they work well with and have a genuine concern for others. The applicant went on to comment on how our students are not cutthroats, unlike those at many other universities. It is, for example, quite rare to hear of one stealing another's untended laptop or sabotaging partners in class projects.

It is our general policy not to give students a preference about what halls they reside in, and we ask few questions about roommate preference. In addition to not segregating athletes, there are no alcohol-free zones nor separate floors for people who want to speak foreign languages in common. We have, of course, equipped some rooms for students in wheelchairs, but we do not hermetically seal off the normally allergic from the ordinary particulates they will encounter anywhere else. We may divide them residentially by sex because we believe they are at an age where their hormones require some down time, but we do not encourage students to separate themselves in living quarters by race, ethnicity, religion, or sexual orientation.

There are few individual rooms with private baths. Notre Dame's residence halls are intentionally communal dwellings that resemble barracks more than high-priced condo units, though we are making modest concessions to demands for more privacy in constructing new ones. Our halls are not merely residences but intended to be Christian communities in which we randomly place people of all sorts together in the hope that they will learn to do more than merely tolerate those who are different. We expect that they will become friends with — and dare I say even love — a wide variety of types, including those among whom they would never have deliberately chosen to dwell if given the option on an admissions form.

Our campus boundaries may serve as a protective island, but the residence halls are laboratories for learning about how to deal with others in worlds beyond. Not only do our students overwhelmingly like what they get, but they are better able to cope later by being arbitrarily tossed together during these years with a range of others be they: rich, poor, Catholic, Buddhist, American, Peruvian, gay, straight, athletic, nerdy, brown, white, bubbas, polyglots, animal rights enthusiasts, or deer hunters.

It is striking that less than three percent ask to switch halls in a typical year. Most treasure the experience even if they would have chosen a private en suite apartment as freshmen had the option existed. If we aren't as diverse according to Berkeley's standards, it may be that we have different standards of measurement. We celebrate diversity by forcing our students to share hallways, bedrooms, and johns, then sitting back and watching them love it – mostly.

Like the Rolling Stones said, "You can't always get what you want." One of life's little ironies is that some of the most miserable people on the planet are those who have gotten everything they thought they ever wanted only to wake up one day feeling like the rich young man in the gospel who had everything but was still unfulfilled. It's a terrible thing to always get our way. It's called being spoiled.

I am not surprised to hear of graduates in the months after Commencement sitting in their yuppie apartments with roommates of their own, choosing lamenting the absence of the community to which they had grown accustomed. Our residential philosophy teaches that what we have in common as God's creatures is far more important that the individual genes that differentiate us. It is a traditional Catholic principle to value community even more than personal freedom and teach that rights exist concurrently with an obligation to subsume one's personal preferences for the greater good. Even if they don't grasp all the theological nuances, our graduates later miss the atmosphere that results from those principles being applied in the halls where they have roamed.

Our philosophy results in less pampering and a better capacity for discerning more clearly wants from real needs. They may have money and talent to spare when they arrive, but I am always impressed when some of the most privileged leave realizing that there are more worthwhile ambitions than becoming permanent fixtures of the leisure class. It's good to be humbled, and there are many roads to humility after getting knocked around by randomly assigned peers over the course of three or four years in the same residence hall. A Biggie here doesn't refer to an oversized ego but a regular (if pint-sized) guy who sticks his neck out for his fellow Otters and earns their respect.

My RA applicant astutely connected these dots and went on in his essay to note that "a different mindset is cultivated here through residence hall living that builds and strengthens what we call the 'Notre Dame family.'" I was reassured to receive some confirmation from a professor from England that we still do a reasonable job teaching students of all backgrounds and preferences how to live in the buildings they inhabit and relish the limited time they are given to do so. Needless to say, the RA candidate aced his RA interview several weeks later. He is one who intuitively grasped Father Moreau's concern for cultivating a spirit of Christian community among students. Our residence halls may not be Beatitudinal nirvanas, but they are relatively charitable places, or at the very least, far from housing for cutthroats, and that does constitute a significant part of the Notre Dame mystique.

*   *   *

Most of our residence halls have received significant renovations, but those pale in comparison with the dramatic alterations of the campus' footprint since my first trek here. Alumni visitors are quick to comment about the expansion; more than a third of our buildings have been constructed within the last thirty years. Today, visitors sometimes mistake the Gothic bookstore for a church. A $70 million science building was recently completed along with a $64 million performing arts center situated just next to an elegant new main entrance. The administration even spent $11 million to construct a building to house the post office and security department. In addition to 200,000-plus plastic sprinkler heads that operate by automatic timer, the more visible quads are manicured like Louis XIV's gardens. It is quite a contrast with earlier days when landscaping meant mowing the dandelions along with the grass, and the University computer system was a tin box stuffed with index cards in the president's office.

Even apart from football, Notre Dame has become an industry, the biggest employer in the Michiana area and the primary tourist attraction in Indiana. It has also become a favorite target of sportswriters and other critics nationwide who view it as the Wal-Mart of American college athletic programs and can't decide whether to root for us or condemn our success. Some of us who live here share those mixed feelings from time to time, but we generally have a broader perspective about the place. We try to remember that it is an academic institution first and a national symbol second.

While our students are more accomplished academically and grade-conscious than my peers, they are certainly more insecure about their futures. Their paralysis in the face of having so many academic and career options is enhanced by rarely ever having made a decision on their own. Sometimes I wonder if they would know how to squeeze their fingers under the knob of a baseball bat to get the first choice in a pickup ballgame, but it is hard to choose one goal in life when the menu is so long.

They are notoriously commitment shy and not many date, except for hall dances, even though hookups are all too frequent on weekends and they talk about sex much more openly. They haven't grown up indoctrinated with the conviction that missing Sunday Mass is a high-speed train ticket straight to hell, yet most of them show up anyway. The habit also sticks beyond graduation. Our Director of Campus Ministry likes to quote a survey from a few years back revealing that seventy-three percent of Catholic Notre Dame graduates ten years out attend church weekly compared twenty-four percent of their peers. Even ten or twenty points less would be mighty impressive.

Like most alumni who romanticize their own pasts, I mourn the passing of the old Notre Dame while indulging in the benefits of the new one. FedEx/Kinko's, Starbucks, Subway, and Burger King franchises have mostly supplanted quirky, grandmotherly individuals such as Amy, Grace, and Dorothy, but I also admit to abandoning Maxwell House. I am now a decaf, nonfat, cinnamon dolce latte devotee.

During the summer, when the students are mostly gone and the weather like a steamy Carolina swamp, I can walk around too if I prefer in baggy khaki shorts, ND t-shirts, and sandals, and blend in with the tourists and conventioneers. But after the fourth of July, I get antsy and begin looking forward to the arrival of the next year's freshmen. By then, I've caught up on sleep.

There may be something distinctive in serving as rector of the first Catholic residence hall with private rooms in the United States, but, despite changes in landscape and fashion, I have come to see that people aren't that much different whether from city or suburb, post-Nixon or post-Clinton. We all have our sorrows and skeletons, but in between we treasure hopes and memories that give us more together than we would have apart, and within that spectrum, there is a virtually endless parade of entertainment masquerading as tradition.

CHAPTER 4

THIEVES AND ENTREPRENEURS

JUST BEFORE DECEMBER study days a couple years back, I opened an e-mail message from a campus detective. Attached to the e-mail was a video segment. In the attached explanation, the officers believed they had identified the four featured suspects but wanted my confirmation. Sure enough, it was four of my freshmen Otters pilfering a small table from the basement of the student center a little after two in the morning.

I called in a couple of my hall staff members and showed them the tape. It looked like a bad episode of COPS. We all agreed on the ID. It helped that one wore a distinctive red coat and knitted hat with two long strands dangling from it. The two freshmen who were the actual thieves thought they had been exceedingly clever.

They lifted the table, surveyed the room, moved it about ten feet, looked around once more, and without even letting it come to a complete rest, shifted it about ten more feet toward the door. They panned the room once last time, then exited quickly with the table. Unfortunately, they were staring directly at a surveillance camera concealed in the ceiling, and a few of the fifty or so witnesses in the room who were not deceived apparently tattled them out when the investigators produced the video.

I brought my laptop upstairs to the room where two of them lived. I was delighted to place it down on the very table they had absconded with, conveniently sitting right next to the door. I told them I wanted them to take a look at something, asked them to come over, and then hit "Play." After the video finished two minutes and twenty-three seconds later, one of them said, "Yep, that's us alright."

When they had their arraignment over in the Residence Life office, they were smartly dressed and quite well-mannered. I commented to the hearing officer that they were so obviously chagrined I felt like Ward Cleaver watching the Beaver hang his head and admit, "Gee, Dad, I guess I was really stupid." She bit her lip trying not to laugh.

Two of them merely got a warning letter. The two actual thieves were assessed a $50 fine. The minimum sanction is usually $100. It's moments like those where I thank God most of them are merely entertaining and decent at heart. It's hard not to laugh and let them off easy when you get a head-hanging confession instead of a pack of lies or a belligerent attitude. I hold showings of the video periodically as a warning to freshmen but have refused to forward it to the culprits. I'm saving it to present to them as a graduation present.

*　　　　　*　　　　　*

Maybe I'm romanticizing the past, but I think their pranks become less original with every passing year. My own friends built bars with doors that had no handles and were closed by magnets underneath designed to conceal kegs or put them out on balconies a floor above attached by extra long hoses that could be tossed out the window quickly if a staff member started snooping around. The fines are much steeper at $250 for those caught with a keg today. I haven't seen one in a hall since shortly after I was ordained, though a few are still occasionally snuck in, most often during Senior Week prior to Commencement. They are quite prevalent on weekends off campus, especially football Saturdays when "Kegs and Eggs" tailgaters are the first morning stop for many undergraduates. Interestingly, I've yet to hear of a student who ever consumed an egg at one of them when he returns in late afternoon after the game.

But it is impressive that their interest in pilfering road signs hasn't lessened since my friends filled the walls of their rooms in Alumni Hall with them. There are, of course, the bewilderingly humorous ones like, "Low flying geese," which always makes me wonder exactly how state departments of transportation expect drivers to handle a nosedive from a determined flock. Some trophies are random like ones for railroad crossings and speed limits. Signs with one's own last name continue to be highly prized.

Occasionally, I find an orange traffic cone or other borrowed objects in the hallways. One night I heard the ceiling above shaking and walked up to find a maintenance department saw horse used on football weekends to support concession stand tables on the quad looking lonely in the hallway. Apparently, they had been doing hurdles over it but raced back to their rooms by the time I huffed up the stairs. Students steal Christmas trees sometimes too, or even chop them down, though an amateur priest-sleuth can usually follow the trail of culprits who dragged a nine-foot tree through the snow.

When I was a junior road tripping to Purdue for a football weekend, some friends (I'll admit we had spent the last few hours in a bar) spotted a six-foot wooden rabbit hanging from a printing store called Insta-Print or Quick-Print, decided to scale the roof, and knocked it down into the street. We stood there and waited, but they didn't return. We thought they'd wandered off, so a couple of guys who didn't see any sense in leaving it lying in the street grabbed it and cut a mile or so back to the frat house where we were staying, darting through alleys and between buildings every time they saw a set of headlights.

When they got back, it didn't quite fit in their car, so they wrapped a ratty yellow blanket around it, then tied down the trunk hatch. In retrospect, it was really dumb to leave stolen merchandise sticking out of a car that could easily be identified. Luckily, the West Lafayette police must have had bigger fish to fry on a football weekend as ours invariably do here.

When the sign thieves were moving out in spring they didn't want to store the rabbit and so dumped it on the South Quad. It was the day of the annual Blue-Gold football scrimmage in late April. I walked out for dinner later only to witness it propped up against a sprinkler and an alumnus posing next to it with his young son while someone else took a picture. They were both smiling broadly. I assumed they figured it was their good fortune to get photographed with the Alumni Hall mascot.

I didn't see any need to disillusion them and reveal that we were Dawgs, not Bunnies. I also failed to tell him that the reason that my friends didn't return to grab the rabbit that September night was because the owner had been downstairs in the store. When he went outside after hearing noises on the roof, he caught them climbing down, shoved a .38 caliber in their faces, and told them, "If you try to run, I'll blow your heads off. Now go get that sign."

They were not amused to discover that the silly rabbit had escaped into the darkness, and I will never know how they convinced the owner that they really would return it the next day. We stayed for the game but hopped out of town as fast as we could afterward while staying closer to the speed limit than most people that age normally do, nervously watching the unfriendly confines of West Lafayette grow dark in the rearview mirror. We knew that bunny feet protruding from the trunk might be difficult to explain to vigilant highway cruisers, but college students are loath to relinquish their hard-won souvenirs, just as they are to forsake fraternity-like customs misguidedly elevated to the level of "sacred tradition."

There is a difference between dumb, funny college stuff and students getting hurt, but the line grows fuzzy when a prank descends unexpectedly into a dangerous confrontation. I should probably be more appalled at the college tradition of petty theft, but I'm mainly glad when they return uninjured. Whether they have successfully snuck in with new interior furnishings might be a matter worth a comment, but it is less of a priority than whether they've taken a slug in the process of acquiring them.

At the end of the day, there are 151 of them and one of me. I'm badly outgunned; I don't carry a .38, but I try not to waste ammo. If I catch them red-handed, they will get sanctioned with community service hours, working trash detail, or forking over fine money that cuts into their beer fund reserves, but rectors have to use some discretion and choose what they really need to know. Letting go of the little stuff, at least when they're contrite as the Beav and haven't come face-to-face with firearms, can build trust for those times when someone could be hurt. There are moments where you really need a straight answer from a student and don't want him wavering about whether his rector will launch a grenade at him or muster the patience to deal with a situation calmly.

So I alternate between worrying about and laughing at them and sometimes do both simultaneously. It's just the normal dynamic of a rector's days as the semesters pass. That is also a tradition that changes little over time even though it's not always quite so romantic.

*   *   *

I was standing outside my room a few minutes before one, taking a last look down the first floor corridor of Sorin College before heading to bed. Four freshmen, two men and two women I'd never seen before, came walking by. I could tell they were freshmen because they had that glazed-over, "is someone going to come after me for being in their building that I'm walking into for the first time" look about them.

Just as they were stumbling past, one of the young men, who was about 5'4", 115 pounds, and may have shaved once for his high school graduation, turned back and asked me, "Is room 101 where you get the shirts down this way?" He was looking for my miscreant sophomores who were selling illegal t-shirts in advance of the home opener against the Michigan football team several days later.

The other reason I knew they were freshmen was because no upperclassman would have been naïve enough to ask a priest wearing his Roman collar for directions to an illegal shirt bazaar. If they had continued walking forward about ten more feet, they would have crashed directly into the room of our president emeritus, my next door neighbor, Monk, who is approaching thirty years living patiently in the midst of half-crazed Otters.

The foursome's information was somewhat inaccurate. There is no room 101 in Sorin College. However, having overheard a hallway reference to shirt sales earlier that evening – and my instincts from more than a year spent trying to keep the lid on this particularly entertaining group of sophomores – I was certain they were looking for room 103, down the hallway and around to the right. I decided to be helpful, pointed them in the opposite direction, then waited.

Not five minutes later, the four strolled back, carrying blue shirts in their hands, heading toward the front entrance. I was still leaning against the doorframe waiting for them. I smiled in their direction and said, "Have a good night." They smiled back, a little more nervously, I thought than when they went by the first time. "Nice kids," I thought to myself. Then, I went back to my room and hopped into bed.

The next evening, after considering several plans of attack, I took a casual stroll down to 103, which is, not so surprisingly, the infamous Quint party room. As I recall, most of its residents were sitting around casually watching ESPN. The room had seven refrigerators, and its walls were filled top to bottom with posters of nearly bare blonds in "inviting" poses, along with a collection of road signs gathered illegally during nocturnal forays, undoubtedly fueled by something they weren't old enough to purchase legally. I squinted my eyes in a hint of disapproval they probably failed to notice.

Then I plopped myself down on one of their couches like I was simply paying a friendly pastoral visit, scratched my head like a befuddled old poop, and said to the assembled, "You know, I must be the dumbest rector on campus. There have been a whole stream of people walking out of here with illegal t-shirts, and one of them told me they were coming from 101, but there is no such room. I know someone down in this wing (which has only five rooms) is selling the things, but I just can't figure out who it might be. Do I feel *stupid*."

Then I stopped abruptly, raised my right hand to my forehead, closed my eyes like Johnny Carson doing his Carnac routine, and shouted, "Wait! I'm having a vision. I see ... I see ... boxes of illegal blue t-shirts being carried out the door, and I see them every single one of them disappearing by" – I paused to look at my watch – "7:41," it being exactly 6:41 PM at the time. Recovering from my revelation and shaking my head, I continued, "Where did that come from? Imagine that. Well anyway, I think I'd better leave."

I stood up, staggered out like I'd been temporarily blinded by bad moonshine, and returned to my room down the hall. A few minutes later one of them came down, knocked on my door, entered hesitantly, and said, "Um, Father Jim, um, I think if you look out your window you'll see us – I mean those bad kids who were selling those illegal shirts – carrying them down the steps."

"Oh, really?" I responded, "Well, thanks for letting me know." Typical Notre Dame students. I was pleased. I gave them an hour, but once again my overachievers had correctly interpreted their rector's idiosyncrasies and exceeded expectations.

The next night I was sitting out on one of our two front porch swings. A wide front porch can be a significant advantage. A rector can pick up a lot of what's going on in his building just watching people come and go, pretending to be doing nothing in particular, though I've started doing crosswords as a good way to appear occupied. It's especially helpful when they come bounding out the door talking about where the off-campus party is that night and stop abruptly when they realize who's sitting there. I play dumb and don't say anything, preferring to leave them deluded that I'm only a short hop away from needing a Miracle-Ear.

As I swung contentedly, four different groups of doe-eyed freshmen came up the front steps within a half hour. The first two groups asked me if I knew where they could buy the shirts. I kept a straight face and told them that it was a mistake: "Someone gave you bad information. The shirts are being sold out of 103 Stanford Hall," I said, just a few minutes walk away on North Quad. The next two groups I didn't even let reach the door before asking them, "Are you looking for the shirts?" When they said yes, I sent them to Stanford too with the same line. They turned right around. From watching the direction they took, all apparently bought it. I was amused as I imagined the confusion that was about to envelop whoever lived in 103 Stanford.

I wondered whether Father Tom, the Stanford rector, might run into these potential buyers and go busting into that room hoping to find illegal merchandise that wasn't there. I left it to fate and never said a word to him, but a few days later I felt no lingering guilt pangs when I discovered that another group was actually selling the same t-shirts out of his hall too, if not necessarily from the same numbered room.

Students and a good number of parents too were still pounding on the door of 103 on game day asking for the shirts, which shows how widely and indiscriminately word had spread about the operation. As the customers kept coming, the occupants knew I had done them a favor, though I don't recall ever receiving a thank you card. Had they been found out by authorities higher up in the command chain than I, their merchandise would have been confiscated, and each would have paid a fine of at least $250. I was content to get the shirts out from under my roof and let them run the risks inherent in running an illegal business out of a car trunk in a campus parking lot.

A student I knew in Morrissey Hall about twenty years ago got nabbed hawking illegal outerwear. Between the loss of his merchandise and fines assessed by the Office of Residence Life, he forfeited the cost of a decent used car. He is now doing quite well, happily married with delightful, apparently well-bred, churchgoing children. I look forward to the day when his first Irish lad comes up the main drive for his freshman year. I'm fond of telling my friends whose children are now arriving in droves: "They're going to do *everything* you did."

Sometimes it pays to keep your charges out of trouble and store up a few chits to bargain with in the future though, oc-casionally, they do challenge one's patience. Or perhaps it's just part of the Sorin tradition to recognize that the entrepreneurial spirit of Rockne and Dorais still endures as part of college life here. However, a couple of years later when we hosted Michigan again, I noticed that a disproportionate of mine had once again started appearing in the same model shirt. I called in one of the likely vendors and told him in-hall shirt sales were history. The tradition of merchandise sales from that same room had become far too obvious. Besides, I was slightly disappointed to hear that they had only made about $600 profit. I suggested they take more Marketing classes.

*   *   *

A few days after the t-shirt boxes' spontaneous exodus that first year of operations, I received a phone call from the equip-ment manager for the Notre Dame football team. He informed me that a student of mine rushing the field after the Michigan game had grabbed a wide receiver's gold football helmet, surrounded himself with a phalanx of classmates, eluded a troop of security personnel in hot pursuit, and dashed out the stadium tunnel, trophy triumphantly in hand. He also incorrectly identified the room, this time as the "first floor quad," and told me the student's name first name was Jim when it was actually another three letter nickname starting with 'J.'

Since he had the last name correct, there was no difficulty divining that the so-called quad was again a reference to the Quint. Not so coincidentally, it was also "Jim" who had knocked on my door five days earlier to inform me about the shirts escaping out the front door. Apparently, the girlfriend of a student manager had been one of the hundreds Jim had bragged to about his prize acquisition. Word was passed along to the team equipment manager who informed me that he would be content with the helmet's return — but would be quite happy to bring down the full weight of the football office's wrath upon all the room's occupants were it not recovered.

I called Nick, the first floor RA, down to my room about 11:15 that night. The previous spring I had announced that I was moving an RA next door to the Quint. There was considerable consternation that the new monitor would cramp a multitude of the room's "traditions," like cracking the ceiling of the freshmen down below. The troops were markedly unenthusiastic about the change. I sat Nick down and told him about the phone call. He nodded his head sheepishly and admitted, "Yeah, the guys were passing it around the room and showed it to me." My decision to station an RA as watchman next door was quickly becoming validated, though subsequently I have encouraged staff members to share information with me more promptly.

"That's exactly what I thought," I said, "and this is what we're going to do. I'm going on my nightly rounds at exactly 12:05 AM I'll be back twenty minutes later. When I come back, there had better be a gold football helmet sitting on my chair or someone is going to get his butt kicked from here to Toledo."

I headed out my door on cue and looked to the left only to see three heads peeking at me from around the corner. One of them was Jim's. I walked down the stairs directly across from my room out of view, left my door open, and waited. I couldn't quite see them from below, but I could detect flashbulbs going off and knew that they were taking turns putting on the helmet and taking pictures. I continued, slowly patrolling along the other three floors before returning from the other direction.

I returned to my room about 12:30. There were several people, including Jim hanging around outside my room. I walked inside and lo! There was a gold football helmet sitting on my chair, so I stood in the doorway and proclaimed loudly, as if I had witnessed the star shining in the East, "Oh! Look at this. There is a real gold Notre Dame football helmet sitting on my chair. How did that ever get there?" Jim just peeked in, shook his Irish head impishly, and said, "Search me but isn't that something?"

A couple of the RAs then came by, so we closed the door, and

I took pictures of them wearing the helmet too. After they left, I locked up, went into my bedroom, placed a Christmas snowman and manger scene on the top of my dresser, sat down directly in front of it, put on the helmet, held a camera out at arms' length, and took a picture of myself smiling broadly. I pasted it into my Christmas letter that year.

The first people I sent it to in December were Jim's parents with whom I developed a very good understanding. They love both their sons dearly but have never imagined that they are princes who can do no wrong. Most parents understand that getting nabbed in a small matter can inoculate their children from incurring worse damage later. Ours generally like to know that someone with a little life experience is watching over them ready to employ discipline, humor, or pure shame depending upon the merits of the situation. I try to keep in mind another wise saying of Father Moreau: "An indulgence prudently managed is worth much more than outbursts and the punishments that follow them."

CHAPTER 5

BE SAFE OR BE GOOD?

MARIJUANA AND DRUG USE HERE IS FAIRLY NEGLIGIBLE, and the hard stuff operates low on the radar screen within a secretive subculture. Most estimates place the number of pot users somewhere between five to ten percent and the hard-core ones a miniscule fraction. Occasionally, there is a spike, usually when one or two students go into business as suppliers. For a while we may have had more people with online poker addictions than serious drug problems, but that fad appears to have leveled off.

The downside is that alcohol is the drug of choice. Every year with metronomic consistency, more than three-quarters of our disciplinary problems are alcohol-related. Fortunately, the number of non-drinkers has significantly increased since my college years when a first attempt at a campus-wide alcohol free party attracted fifteen people and universal scorn. Today, despite the bingers, there is more tolerance for peers who make better choices.

That theory received some confirmation during my first year in Sorin College. I meet one-on-one with all the freshmen in

71

the first month of the first semester. One told me about walking into a room full of sophomores in early September where most of the crowd was shotgunning beers (punching a hole in the bottom with a can opener, then pulling the top). He didn't drink at all, and one of the residents tried to hand him a beer. I was relieved to hear him say, "I told the guy I don't drink, and he just said 'That's cool.'"

It's one thing for students to drink and another for them to drink too much too often. Trying to stop it entirely is akin to eliminating sin – an admirable goal but progress is inevitably gradual. My cardinal rule that I hammer home relentlessly is that no one should be forced into anything he (or she) doesn't want to do because it is peer pressure coupled with drinking competitively or ritually that causes most of the serious trouble.

The University did ban hard alcohol, anything over fourteen percent, entirely from campus several years back, regardless of whether students were of legal age. Many of the worst cases stemmed from inexperienced drinkers quaffing various forms of spiked kool-aid, clueless about its alcohol content. Since the policy tightened up, more head to off-campus houses to drink, but that has been counterbalanced by a falloff in the number of bad cases, almost two-thirds fewer hospital runs the first year the policy was implemented.

Our country once discovered that Prohibition created more problems than it solved. We could stand piously on legalisms and wash our hands of responsibility by banning alcohol entirely, but hall staff members are a lot more likely to find out who has an actual drinking problem that we can help if we're not lurking around the corner ready to pounce on casual usage. While staff and students' opinions about precisely where to draw those lines in the sand naturally tend to vary, the goal is to create an atmosphere where our charges can expect us to act rationally and differentiate between what is and is not problematic behavior. I wish we could emulate the more practical Europeans who train their kids how to appreciate alcohol from a young age rather than treating it like demon rum and turning it into a bigger temptation later.

Rev. Theodore Hesburgh, C.S.C, our other president emeritus, tells a story about twenty-five-year-old veterans returning from World War II and living in Badin Hall under those earlier draconian rules designed for eighteen year olds. Getting caught with booze on campus could have gotten them suspended. As he said, "How can you tell a guy who spent four years getting shot at that he can't have a belt when he wants one?"

So he walked the hallways one night and told them all to hand over whatever they had stashed away. They were skeptical but reluctantly did as they were ordered. Then he told them, "I'm keeping it in my room from now on. When you feel the need for a belt, come down and I'll give it to you." His priority was to keep them *out* of trouble, not to follow all the fine print of the rulebook mindlessly. Also, he undoubtedly realized that, under his supervision, the atmosphere in his parlor would likely deter them from having too many.

Ours are, admittedly, a little younger, but Notre Dame's alcohol policy still strives to balance legal responsibility with some degree of pragmatism. We inform students that they are obliged to obey the law, but, as I say to parents during orientation, "I'm not going to bust an eighteen year old for sitting in his room having a beer while watching a football game when most of you would hand him one at home." We focus on people who are creating problems rather than busting those going thirty-five in a thirty-mile-per-hour zone.

In our favor, we don't have a Greek system and since social life revolves around the halls, neither do we have a huge problem with formal initiation rites. We haven't had deaths from ritual drinking in our dorms like fraternities elsewhere, though we've had a few from people leaving off-campus parties over the last several decades. Residence halls do continue to have issues with "Disorientation" exercises, upperclassmen gathering freshmen together on the sly during their first week, taking them to off-campus houses, plying them with booze, and sharing their grievously flawed "wisdom" about how to drink without getting caught by enemy rectors. We've had some success in squashing the more egregious of those, though they tend to reignite periodically like smoldering brush fires. I'm glad that the culture in Sorin College is laid-back enough that most of the older guys aren't forcing people to chug beers their first week of college, but I'm not dumb enough to think that many won't succumb to more subtle forms of peer pressure later on.

A couple of years ago I read a rector evaluation from a student who wrote, "Father King doesn't seem to realize that college is all about drinking and picking up girls. If he thinks he's going to do anything to change ONE person's mind, he's just kidding himself." I took it as a compliment. At least my bosses knew I was trying. I wonder if that's what he'll tell his kids thirty years from now when he's footing the tuition bills.

In fact, we have changed the atmosphere here over time by persistent education, tighter enforcement of public intoxication, targeting hard liquor, and a major investment in facilities and programming designed to promote viable alternatives to alcohol. There are many more people who don't drink, and there has been a vast expansion in the range of attractive non-alcoholic programming since the 1970s. In the short-term, we may not change one person's mind about anything; over the long-haul we outlast them and plug away at changing the culture, ratcheting up our expectations a bit more each year. A week is an eternity for a college student, but those of us who are permanent residents measure progress in years and decades.

Some just fall in with the wrong crowd, and that's why my twelfth commandment during orientation is about making the right friends. More people get in trouble because of who they are with than because of what they're doing on their own. Others arrive here leaning the wrong way too. The interesting thing about the rector evaluations is that more comment favorably about our attempts to create a safe, livable environment than rant about their inalienable rights to enjoy hookups and hooch. I just wish they felt less inhibited about expressing their actual preferences when they're mouthing off with one another at the dining hall.

*   *   *

Many early encounters with freshmen do lead them in the aftermath, if not along a path of complete sinlessness or total abstinence, further away from trouble that would land them in a conference with a disciplinary hearing officer in the Golden Dome. Wising up enough to avoid detection may not be a Christian's ultimate destination, but it's a useful rest stop for a college student on the long road to virtue.

One year I got a report from a rector of a North Quad hall that one of mine had been caught by a graduate student AR (assistant rector) throwing up in someone's sink and tried to run away when confronted. When I called him in and asked what happened, he was evasive at first, minimizing what had happened: "I wasn't that drunk. He just told me to leave. I did what he told me. He said nothing was going to happen."

Then I asked, "Do you remember throwing up in the sink?" Then I read the incident report, quoting it in full. Five minutes later, he was suffering the full effects of guilty mortification, kicking himself because he wasn't ordinarily the type to lie. "Did God ever make a bigger fool than me?" he asked. Over the next two days, he went looking for that rector five times to apologize before finally catching up to him. He was kicking himself so badly, I halved his community service sanction because as I told him, "Look, between multiple trips rector hunting and spending hours in between feeling like an ax murderer, you've already worked off about five hours. Lighten up."

Another one was heading toward the stadium on game day from a parking lot tailgater with a guy who could barely stand.

That didn't stop the one who was plowed from randomly smacking a tailgating alumnus south of the basketball arena. He landed in jail after a couple of the alum's classmates knocked him down and kicked him in the kidneys for sport. The old Domers all got off without so much as a parking ticket.

On the other hand, Jack, who had tried to break up the melee, stuck around and got nabbed by the police when they drove up and started breathlyzing everyone. He had only consumed two beers, but he was nineteen. His mom was furious when she found out he'd been cited. She had spent the previous eighteen years telling Jack to pick his friends wisely before dropping him off with me and had been pleased to hear my commandments. I have developed a very warm relationship with her too. We talk a similar language. Not surprisingly, Jack stayed off the police scanner until he graduated.

*   *   *

Another rector told me this story from about five years ago. Pat made a bet with his roommates during a drinking game called quarters. As the loser, he had to make a loop of the South Quad naked. Unfortunately, he had the misfortune of starting his race as two campus police officers on bicycles were converging from both ends. Neither did it help that his running skills were slightly impaired.

So, the following night, he walks into the rector's room, looking a little sheepish. When the rector explained to Pat that he could be up on three separate charges: public intoxication, running from a police officer, and indecent exposure, he looked up,

77

cheeks flushing, hung his head downward, looked up again and said, "I wasn't really trying to run from the cops. I was just trying not to be naked."

After that comment, the rector had to make an effort not to bust out in a chortle. Before his disciplinary conference at the Office of Residence Life a week later, he related the account of this dialogue to his hearing officer. Again, she understood, and there was more lip-biting. He wasn't charged with either indecent exposure or evading arrest, but he did get nailed for intoxication. Our students may complain about Notre Dame's rules, but I hope they eventually realize it's better to make mistakes in our jurisdiction than in some other where a college prank today can result in a sex-offender listing.

It could be that, like my literary hero Atticus, we're overly tolerant at times, but that tradition dates back to our founding. The first student known to be tossed from Notre Dame was Willie Ord in 1846. He had repeatedly come back to campus tanked from a South Bend saloon when a single drop of alcohol could cause one to be handed his permanent exit papers. Then one night, he returned to campus about midnight and became the first documented case of a drunken student jumping into St. Mary's Lake, also in the skin God fashioned for him.

The faculty board recommended expulsion, but Father Sorin, like his mentor Moreau, was a relative softy who didn't buy into the hickory stick approach typical of the nineteenth century. He wanted to give Willie one more chance, and the founder always got his way. A few weeks after Willie's reprieve, he got loaded again and slugged a professor, and even Sorin had enough. One hopes, however, that young Willie somewhere down the line realized that he had been given every possible chance, every last bit of rope from people who wanted him to leave with a Notre Dame degree.

*   *   *

I'm not so concerned that students experiment and inevitably face a learning curve about alcohol endemic to their age group. It's the unstable rocket fuel combination of alcohol and sex on public display that differentiates the MTV culture of the Millennial Generation from mine. People of every age, especially collegians, have been getting drunk and falling into bed with one another since Adam and Eve were expelled from Paradise. They've usually regretted it later.

We went to bars and keg parties off-campus, and people occasionally darted around campus naked in the '70s too. While I recall leaving Alumni Hall for bars selling cheap quarter beers, I don't remember heading off-campus for ABC (anything but clothes) parties where males and females alike show up wrapped in duct tape, bubble wrap, or pieces of cardboard placed strategically over sensitive body parts. I heard a student last year at a Student Affairs presentation say that she thought Notre Dame students were less inclined to disrobe publicly under the influence than at other universities but not quite as much as people like me would hope. That's probably right. I'm glad that our students discern some behavioral differences from peer institutions, but more of them head to beaches for spring break hoping to get on MTV than we would prefer.

Neither do I quite know what to do with the posters of blond

79

girls making out with one another that hang in some rooms. Farrah Fawcett alone in a swimsuit was quite enough for an earlier generation of Alumni Dawgs. It's easy enough to order hard-core porn taken down, but that's rare. It is the new variations on the soft-core variety that leave me confused about where we should draw our lines in the sand. I can find examples even in the rooms of some of our more wholesome, church-going Otters. They aren't much of a stretch from what we can all see wandering by an Abercrombie and Fitch store window.

I sometimes think I should do more than raise eyebrows and archly comment, "That's interesting" when I encounter them. Then again, I can't remember one being hauled down before a parental visit either, even though I have suggested that when I know that Mom and Dad are heading into town. Mostly, I suspect that we are so overwhelmed with constantly swimming upstream against the pervasive vulgarity of our culture that we have become too immune to it. Parents and rectors alike are lost wondering where to differentiate between natural expressions of normal, late adolescence preoccupations and capitulating entirely to the realization that even if we rip their posters, they can turn on their flat screen TVs and view worse on standard cable channels.

When I was a freshman in high school, a religious brother from the discipline office came into our classroom to tell us a story about a miscreant young man. He had fallen into petty crime and promiscuous behavior. One day he was getting chased by the police after breaking into a car and stealing a stereo. He ran through a backyard trying to elude arrest and vaulted over a wooden fence. In his haste, he failed to notice a rusty nail at the top. When he jumped down, the nail caught on his pants and ripped off his testicles. I am sure it was apocryphal, and after he left the room we all sniggered. Despite the prevalence of sex everywhere, I suspect we fear that talking about it will make us sound like the ninnies of our own generation. However, I have to admit, thirty-five years later I still remember the brother's gory tale.

Often good old-fashioned, understated shame from a guy in a collar succeeds in making them reflect a bit more than they would otherwise. Life is a series of choices between whether to confront directly or nudge gently. It's possible to say something without humiliating people or censoring every wall hanging. I don't like to pile on with those who are making more good choices than lousy ones if it's nothing more than hormones flaring up normally, but this world, where the roughest pornography can be accessed with a couple of mouse clicks, is certainly a different one from where I grew up with friends hiding *Playboys* in the rafters of parents' unfinished basements. As a general rule, I prefer nudges to humiliation or finger-pointing lectures and hold more deliberate forms of guidance in reserve for those seriously tanking.

A generation ago, before Mothers Against Drunk Driving (MADD) and later the student version SADD were founded, our society had a "What can you do about kids being kids?" attitude toward loaded teenagers crashing into light poles at ninety miles an hour. Then those groups started agitating for higher drinking ages and tougher laws to combat alcohol-related deaths. The phrase "designated driver" entered the lexicon, and a lot more of ours these days have been successfully indoctrinated to call a cab rather than drive drunk. The number of alcohol-related deaths has actually declined over those years as a result of a dramatic change in legal policy and societal attitudes.

We need to develop the same consciousness and energy about sexual attitudes and conduct, even if we can expect to garner less support from legislatures for limitations on public displays. A couple of years ago I complained to a University official that we were mandating a one-hour educational session on homosexuality for our freshmen but doing nothing about the topic of sexuality in general. The Millennials are about the most tolerant generation in the history of the world when it comes to accepting difference of race, religion, and sexual orientation. We are at the position of decreasing marginal returns from beating them over the head with more sensitivity workshops. Our generation needs the instruction more.

There is a student in my hall who always says, "Be good" instead of "See you later" whenever he passes by me. Mike says he got it from his father. I usually don't give it a second thought, but the reminder to be good is the shorthand version of something Father Moreau wrote about persevering in virtue. Unfortunately, our institutions of higher learning have become more intent since I left college on advising students to be careful than calling upon them to become champions of goodness.

Abortions have been declining slowly in the U.S., but as the number of sexually transmitted diseases continues to rise among this age group nationally, I regret that the ethics of our contraceptive-minded culture has stagnated at the level of "Don't get pregnant." College students today are prolonging marriage and are more afraid of pregnancy interfering with their career paths than their parents were in the early days of the Sexual Revolution. They are more likely than others their age to use birth control, but another response has been to opt more frequently for oral sex in the delusion that anything short of intercourse isn't sex and is therefore safe.

It's interesting that STDs are increasing in colleges and universities that, unlike Notre Dame, do dispense condoms freely. I think we're right to encourage our students to "Be good" rather than merely "Be safe." We are obliged to do what we can to elevate their minds toward the heavens and out of the gutter. They may not listen to us as much as we'd like immediately, but after hitting a few speed bumps, more of our warnings begin to resonate than cynics playing to their worst impulses and short-changing their potential for virtue believe possible.

One weekend after another, the most pressing issue of sexuality on campus is the hundreds of casual encounters that are scarring people who wind up at the health or counseling center afterward because they have been trained to believe that sex can be fun with little risk. One wonders about how glad those who entered into what is known as a "friends with benefits" relationship will be to see one another at future alumni reunions. I don't object to open discussion of AIDS and STDs or more education about "plumbing" at an earlier age. However, we can't simply throw up our hands, assume that college students will have sex regardless of what we tell them, urge them to be careful, and neglect to teach them about the sanctity of their bodies. I am pleased that there are more students on campus pressing us to discuss Pope John Paul II's "theology of the body," but there are many less vocal who would appreciate the support if we talked about it more.

Some of the biggest headlines out of the University in the last several years, aside from the athletic variety, reported a debate over whether to allow The Vagina Monologues to take place on campus. It's not the central point at all. The real news is that too many of our kids are being harmed by casual attitudes toward all kinds of sex, and we are too hesitant about challenging them to use their bodies in a manner that respects their innate tendency toward goodness. I have never had a student tell me that I spoke too much about sexual issues from the pulpit, but some have told me they hear too little from us about them. It may be that clergy are too self-conscious about being ridiculed earlier for the Church's teaching on birth control and more lately for its representatives' own sexual misdeeds. But it's not just priests or Catholic schools that are forfeiting the high ground.

In February 2007, Notre Dame sponsored a forum called *"Sex in the City of God."* Students came to watch an episode of the television show with a slightly abbreviated name followed by a panel discussion with professors, students, and a priest. It's a start. Those are conversations we need to have more frequently, publicly and privately with our undergraduates. I suspect that when we get a better grip on how to engage in dialogues with them, the puerile fascination with "Monologues" will naturally decline to a more appropriate level of importance in the campus' collective consciousness.

Sex, like drinking, we will always have with us on campus, but I would like to think that we can make some progress on what they do with one another as we have with alcohol issues. Dealing with college drinking is like trying to eliminate an ant hill by stepping on it. It's frustrating, but we're engaged in the battle because while most overindulgence simply causes growing pains, other times the scars never heal.

The wounds from casual promiscuity are less obvious but can be more enduring. Even if we are exasperated because we can't filter out the degrading messages screaming at our kids from televisions, computers, and print ads, we need to jump into the muck and teach and preach more than we do to lessen its impact. To do that which is seemingly futile in the eyes of skeptics is, in its barest expression, simply the life's work of every Christian. We have to trust that the individual successes we encounter from the effort make our tilting at windmills seem a little less impractical.

CHAPTER 6

IT GOES AS THEY GO

THE BEST RAS are nothing like me. They are laid back, cheerful, and indifferent about whether friends wander in, plop down on their couches, inhale their food, and borrow their X-Boxes. I'm pretty good about leaving my door open, though it does pain me to watch a whole troop spill imitation cheddar cheese all over my carpet and ground it in with their dirty bare feet whenever I cook chili for them.

The stellar RAs spend more time in other students' rooms than their own and can study in one where six other people are screaming at one another while playing video games. They are breezily nonchalant and worry about little. While they are usually more mature than the general population – which is why they get hired to be role models in the first place – they share their peers' sense of invulnerability. Then again, they inhabit an age bracket that can eat four slices of Papa John's thick crust pizza every night at 11:00 PM and lose weight.

I'm not sure I had ever heard of an RA when I arrived at Notre Dame, but I was glad to know that there was a senior a couple doors down looking out for us. I didn't expect him to take me and two classmates along on a road trip to a football game in Mississippi three weeks into the school year. Neither did I anticipate that he would be the student representative for Miller Brewing on campus though we did appreciate the free beer signs he provided for us. It is another example of how times have changed that we now exercise tighter control over role models' secondary employment.

One of the best RAs I ever knew had a long ponytail almost down to his belt and wore an earring before so many college students starting turning themselves into human pincushions. He was dry, spoke in a low monotone, and was an Episcopalian teetering on the edge of Buddhism. He was slightly puzzled by Catholics and their rules so questioned everything institutional but gently and respectfully. His demeanor tranquilized agitated people like a double dose of Valium. He told me less than he probably should have but everything that was important for me to know.

That same year, I fired another RA that I'd inherited from a previous rector in mid-April. We'd had problems and run-ins all year long. He questioned most things I said with a superior attitude. One night when there was trouble brewing, I went looking for him. He was supposed to be on duty; his books were in the study lounge, and his glasses on top, a classic maneuver by someone who didn't realize we've seen that ploy before. I asked a number of students if they'd seen him. No one had a clue or, interestingly enough, attempted to provide him with any cover as students are wont to do for the ones they respect. If he'd admitted his mistake, I wouldn't have let it go, but instead I got slammed with a lecture about everything I had been doing wrong all year. It was the proverbial final straw.

I did tell him that he could remain in his room for the last few weeks. I had no desire to humiliate him and would make no announcement that he'd been fired. He stomped out of my room. Forty-five minutes later his mother knocked on my front door, and the first words out of her mouth were, "I can't believe you would do such a thing to my son. How can you live with yourself as a Catholic priest?"

When I responded, "Actually, very easily, ma'am," she stomped away too – like mother, like son – and that was the last I saw of either. After they both departed I found out a number of interesting things about that RA from other residents who didn't appreciate the fact that he had broken a number of rules while allowing his buddies, though not others who weren't, to do likewise.

*   *   *   *

A few years later in another hall, I discovered that two of my RAs had been ticketed by a police officer for illegal drinking the night before the Tennessee game in Knoxville. When neither failed to mention this to me nine days later, despite the fact that their indiscretion was grounds for job forfeiture, I held them back at the end of a staff meeting and asked, "Now when exactly were you going to tell me about getting busted at the Tennessee game?"

They both hung their heads rather Beav-like, and one said,

"Yeah, I guess we forgot to mention that." Understanding their predicament in getting caught red-handed, they groveled appropriately. I asked them each to schedule separate hour-long one-on-ones with me. When we met, I not only remained calm but was positively cheerful, though the time passed quite slowly for them. I know they weren't sinless either between October and May, but they did turn out to be solid RAs. I didn't let on what a tough haul it would have been if I'd had to replace them.

We had a rector retreat later that year in the spring. The Campus Ministry staff conducting it surprised us with a slideshow. They had surreptitiously contacted our hall staffs, asking for a lethal combination of incriminating pictures and warm fuzzies about what good rectors we all were. These photos and comments were projected onto a screen for all to see, including my boss, Father Poorman.

There were a few funny pictures, but most hall staffs wrote kindly about their rectors. In contrast, my stellar group made a beeline to the sarcasm bin: "When we think about you – Father Jim King – we think about a man of consistency, a man of integrity, and a man with an incredibly limited array of clothing. You are the only man who can call one of your residents a midget and raise his body image . . . You are excellent at listening to our opinions, even if it sometimes seems that you are equally gifted at doing the exact opposite of what we recommend . . . You have brought order and peace to a land that was once ruled by savages … You've taught us to pick our battles and to keep our eye on the big picture."

They were surprised that I framed their letter and put in on my bookshelf, but reading between the lines of the remarks about midgets, my mostly black wardrobe, and their crummy advice, I treasured the backhanded compliments. College-age males don't hit many direct forehands in the warm fuzzy department. I thought that maybe even the two I could have had fired appreciated our fruitful one-on-ones the previous fall. Aside from the tone and some slight exaggerations, they were right about everything they wrote. I did tell them to pick their battles and did listen to them – some of the time. The letter also revealed that I am making some progress in contrast to my earlier critic who told me I would never change even one savage's mind about anything.

*   *   *

A limited but accurate one-word summary of another one of those authors would be "cocky." My initial one-on-one supervisory session with Matt during his RA year was not the first time I felt compelled to share that observation with him. He was also one of the few students at ND who caused insurance companies to lose money on stitches and casts. When he unexpectedly appeared at my door on crutches in April, it may not have been the approved pastoral care response, but I just laughed. We conspired initially to keep the news from his mom, who was worried about the insurance people bailing on him, although he later broke down and 'fessed up. I found out from her later that it was his usual pattern to call home and spill all the beans only after the worst had passed. Luckily, that ankle injury was just a sprain even if looked like a clubbed foot for three days.

A few months earlier, Matt went to the Fiesta Bowl with mono and spent most of three days lying in a hotel bed. The illness put a serious crimp in his training for the Bengal Bouts, Notre Dame's charity boxing tournament in mid-February. The doctor at home told him, "No strong physical exertion for a month."

Less than two weeks after the bowl game, I saw Matt heading to boxing practice. I said, "And you're not going to tell the club doctor about what the one at home said?"

"Nope," he answered definitively. A couple of days later, he did a thousand pushups. I might have ripped the gloves off a dewy freshman, but given my inclination to avoid minor battles, I was not about to sidetrack a willful twenty-one year old senior who feels deprived unless he's popping Vicodin or soaking cracked bones in buckets of ice from getting his nose smashed in the ring.

Matt went to Uganda to work in the Holy Cross missions too, for sixteen months after graduation. He survived a double bout of typhoid and malaria and a motorcycle accident in which he and the bike's driver single-handedly stopped a bank robber by colliding head on with his getaway car as bullets rained overhead between his slower accomplices and the police. Of course, he could have easily avoided the whole situation simply by following the instructions given to all overseas volunteers explicitly forbidding them from hitching rides on bike taxis since our insurance won't cover the damage. Unfortunately, the brain chip for following orders shorts out frequently. Not surprisingly, Matt did not seek out medical assistance for his twisted knee, busted up ankle, or grapefruit-sized swelling on the elbow. Neither his parents nor I were surprised by the accident or his response to it. Months later, I wrote to him that he may live to be ninety-five, but he'll be hobbling around with ninety percent bionic parts.

Matt eventually encountered larger frustrations. The only thing more ironic than a white kid from Houston teaching Ugandan high schoolers about the "Cotton South" – because geography questions appear on national SAT-type tests based upon that bit of outdated information – would be if a black kid from Alabama had to do it. It was more unnerving to teach in schools without textbooks and watch helplessly as busloads of students were booted out and sent home because they couldn't afford $50 tuition bills.

However, after a few months of indulging generalized rage about the injustice of third world poverty, he also learned that it's easier to spew forth knee-jerk reactions than to formulate complex solutions. Oppressed people don't always want well-meaning outsiders' help; paltry income levels are not a blanket excuse for drunken soldiers' brutality; and bushel loads of cash from America won't magically eliminate a culture of pervasive corruption. Matt also discovered something about his vocation working at St. Jude's and Lakeview Secondary School – a natural gift for teaching. During his senior year, I'd tried to tell him walking off the field after an interhall football game that he had a flair for coaching like no twenty-one year old I'd ever seen. I suggested that he would find his niche in that and/or in teaching, but some things they have to find out for themselves.

I first locked horns with Matt when he was an even cockier

seventeen year old. After a few years getting banged up more than usual, surviving an RA year where his rector barked at him repeatedly (always for good reason), and becoming a one-man disease host in Africa, he painted in many of the gaps in his own bigger picture. Some of those lessons came the hard way, but some people, even RA role models, make a habit of asking for it.

*   *   *

There are those who are compliant and others more hard-headed, but in whatever form they come, the people who really run the hall – any hall – are the RAs. I tell them at the beginning of the year, "The year goes as you go," and it does. I also let them know that it's more important for them to be on the same page and not undercut one another more than it is for them to follow my party line to the letter. Students expect me to be tougher than an undergraduate senior. No matter how many excellent speeches they hear about their fiduciary responsibilities as official residence life representatives, even the best of them aren't quite ready to be as hard-nosed as the book says.

That was borne out with Matt and his bunch. I only received one minor complaint about any of them the entire year and that at year's end. Most people who have worked in residence life for a while will say that it takes three years for a hall to become your own. After that, both hall staffs and residents have figured out a rector's idiosyncrasies and how to work with or around them.

I was even more fortunate the following year to have four RAs whose names were never entered into a southern police department's police blotter. They rarely drank MGDs on duty, and none of them ever forgot what bar he left his car at the night before. I never felt compelled to run upstairs and check things out because of a vague uncertainty that they hadn't just interpreted the rulebook loosely but used it as kindling.

Outside my door is a board for staff nameplates. Each duty night, the RA posts his name along with that of the head staff person, either me or an assistant rector on call. The first night in August, the RA assigned to be on that evening posted his name above mine. That had never happened in the previous three years, and while I was amused, I also thought it took a little gall. It set the pattern for the year. They did run the dorm – very well indeed. My recliner got a lot more wear my fourth year, providing comfort to a body with a mind much more at ease and a bit preoccupied trying to churn out a book about them. Tony, Tim, Sush, and Greg proved eminently capable of running our little asylum with little help from me. I was bemused and pleased that they had merited my confidence and begrudged them not their preeminent place in the staff pecking order because I'd never lived for a year in a hall with fewer problems. But it takes a while to build the kind of trust that makes it possible for people like me to know what we need to and keep students from serious harm.

*   *   *

My assistant rectors feel free enough to tell me with some regularity that they are the most overpaid employees on campus. I inevitably agree with them. They start out with a $14,000 salary, free room and board, and about $5,000 in tuition credits. Most ARs are second- and third-year law students, but some are enrolled in other graduate programs.

One of mine is assigned to supervise hall government, monitor orientation weekend, and manage the monthly duty schedule. The other takes care of maintenance issues, assigns community service workers, logs student info into the computer system a few times a year, and works with me on religious programming. They both sit in on disciplinary meetings.

Beyond that I have a hard time coming up with other specific responsibilities. Their main one is simply to share duty nights so rectors don't drive themselves nuts sitting around every night waiting for something to go wrong. I tell them that I want them to be the "RAs for the RAs," the person an RA turns to when he doesn't want to share a piece of information with me. They run interference, and they provide another set of eyes to make sure the RAs don't stray too far. It was one of them who told me about the bust at Tennessee.

I generally prefer to hire assistant rectors who were not undergraduates here. Most of them serve for two years and sometimes three. I've known too many ND grads who grew bored by the time they had finished living six or seven years in a residence hall, especially when it's the same one. Others have a hard time separating themselves emotionally from their undergraduate days when they return to the scene of their former petty crimes. I've been fortunate to find some who attended other schools and value the opportunity to enjoy a taste of Notre Dame life without taking it for granted.

One of the best ways to figure out whether a staff member is doing his or her job in a residence hall is to mentally log how often they stop by to check in and share information with us that they don't necessarily have to. There are people who show up for duty nights and do the minimum but never grasp that we bosses assess them not only by what they report but what they omit in comparison to their predecessors. The idea that "If we don't say anything, he won't know," is a delusion, and people entering the workforce should consider that there are bosses out there smarter than stay-at-home priests. It takes some patience for a rector to build a case and wait for the right educational moment, but there are life lessons better learned here than in some other ogre's workplace.

I've never terminated a student that I've hired to be part of my staff. Perhaps I've been too tolerant at times or simply unwilling to admit I'd made a mistake. I know that I would consider it a personal failure if I had to let one go. I demand loyalty from them, and I would rather bite through my own tongue rather than ditch one of them. It's one of those lessons that I learned growing up back home in my other world before I came to Notre Dame. I was taught at a young age to take care of your own, even if that requires an occasional trip to the woodshed. I may not return to Canaryville often, but there are some fragments of wisdom from an older time of stable parishes and neighborhoods that still endure.

*   *   *

I suppose most universities' residence life officers look for hall staff candidates who will enforce rules and be good programmers. Those aren't my primary concerns at all. I have described the key quality that's needed in various ways: the ones I trust the most; the ones who would act most maturely if rejected; those most respected by peers. I look for certain types that I call shock absorbers: quiet lunch pail guys whatever the family bankroll who don't get easily rattled, aren't on an ego trip, and de-escalate alcohol-fueled conflicts with nineteen year old raging hormones rather than revving up their engines. Time and again the one who almost got left off the list because he was thought to be too quiet ends up the best of the bunch. It also helps if they are regulars at daily Mass. I've found that there is a strong correlation between Mass attendance, personal maturity, fidelity to the job, and enthusiasm for the University's residential mission.

I highlight the qualities I'm looking for in staff members by showing our new hall staffs the first episode of Band of Brothers during training days in August. I want a team of Lieutenant Winters, patient with ordinary human foibles, not martinets like Captain Sobol, revoking weekend passes for an entire company because one paratrooper's bayonet is rusty and another bloused his pants. It's also critical for an RA to have a strong moral compass and a willingness to put other people's needs before one's own. Authority has less to do with knowing rules than with truly knowing one's self.

It gave me special pleasure to give Peter, one of the Tennessee culprits, an award at the end of the year as the best RA, especially since he had been the primary drafter of the letter I had framed. The entire year he repeated at virtually every staff meeting that he was the worst RA and the whole bunch were the lousiest ever. I wrote a letter about him when I recommended him for that award, that read, "People like him, trust him, respect him, and congregate around him more than he realizes." It is how they end up at the year's conclusion that matters more than the tumbles they take the first few weeks on the job. It pays to give them space to earn redemption whenever possible.

The RAs and ARs run the hall one of two ways: with the rector's trust or without it. They are our eyes and ears. That is why I begin cultivating future RAs when they are freshmen. It pains me a little when people who would have made great RAs move off campus, but I understand when their desire to maximize the amount of time they have with friends during their final year becomes their top priority. As their college years pass, they grow increasingly aware of how short that time is.

At most colleges and universities, sophomores and juniors are eligible for resident assistant positions in dorms, filled mostly by freshmen. However, at Notre Dame almost eighty percent of the student body remains on campus for four years, and RA positions are reserved exclusively for seniors. I am convinced that the relative maturity of our RAs is another key reason why we have so few real tragedies in our halls. It's a lot easier for a senior to step up and intervene without fearing their peers' reaction to "getting someone in trouble" than for a sophomore still struggling to learn the college ropes.

Occasionally, some observers of the campus scene will make sloppy remarks about how the residence halls here are like fraternities elsewhere, but it's a weak analogy. As at other colleges and universities, RA's do spend a good amount of time performing mundane tasks – making rounds, filling out room condition reports, checking bathrooms, and just staying up late hanging around – interspersed with bursts of personal crises and confrontations with drunks.

During the interview process, no one ever says they like long hours, getting friends in trouble, or cleaning up Friday night vomit induced by cheap beer, but candidates typically do mention their gratitude for how their own freshman year RA welcomed them to Notre Dame. Almost every applicant says, "I want to give something back" and speaks about wanting to be a big brother or sister for the younger ones.

It's remarkable that so many seniors compete for a position that dumps them into a fishbowl of intense scrutiny from peers and seriously curtails their social lives during their final year. Yet, there is rarely a shortage of applicants. I've often told people that the training and development of RAs is the most distinctive and important manifestation of Notre Dame's educational mission outside the classroom.

It used to be that we had priests or brothers on every floor before coeducation, vocation shortages, and rule changes that made lights-out obsolete. For better or worse, seniors now fill most of those shoes. Though it may not be part of the academic core curriculum, we have an obligation to teach our students how to shepherd others during their hours outside the classroom, and there is no substitute for good hands-on experience.

Many universities have outstanding academics, championship sports teams, and even vibrant campus ministries at those with a religious affiliation. But at Notre Dame, an RA is a partner in ministry, the individual most immediately responsible for the personal welfare of each student. RAs have a duty to know everyone in their halls and to care for them, whatever that may entail, from having lunch with a freshman eating alone to turning in a classmate whose behavior is out of control.

RA applicants approach their senior year with gratitude, wanting to give something back, primarily because others cared enough to know them and form them into a community that became a second home. The main difference between residential life at Notre Dame and most other universities is that the priority here is caring for people, not managing housing. It's what drives life here on those several hundred days each year when the football stadium is empty.

One year I was asked to give a presentation to all the hall staffs after telling my boss about my "Three P's" talk to my own. It's based on one of the lines I have used every year, "If you forget everything else you hear during staff training, remember this: Presence Prevents Problems." In order to be effective, a staff person has to be there, and when he or she is watching, students won't follow through on a good number of temptations that they otherwise would. Even more importantly, our crowd judges rectors and other staff most in the end about whether we care by how much we care to be around.

There is no higher compliment that a rector can give to a student than to say that he or she would make a good RA. A disproportionate number of the weddings and baptisms we are asked to celebrate later come from among our cohort of former ones. They are the ones we come to know best and remain in closest contact with for years afterward because they have shared most in the University's mission of educating the heart as well as the mind.

CHAPTER 7

RECTOR TO RECTOR

IT IS NEARLY IMPOSSIBLE TO DISGUISE minor imperfections, let alone hide major flaws, when you live side by side with intelligent, observant college students. After all, fishing for chinks in the rector's armor is more fun than intramural sports. I know that I was always quick to comment when I thought I'd spotted a few in my rector.

Last year my staff wrote an "ode" called, "Father Jim, Love Hymn" and performed it on Sorin's front porch at our annual talent show. I'm used to dealing with shifty undergraduates and had a sneaking feeling they were going to drag me onstage to listen to it, so just beforehand I slipped out the back door. I ran around to the front of the building and hid behind a sprawling tree halfway across the quad from the front porch where the show was being staged. My favorite verse was:

> *You turn wine into blood*
> *I think that's pretty cool.*
> *You keep the freshmen in line*
> *So they don't break the rule.*

You knew my name before I came here
That made me kinda scared.
But you didn't bust my freshman party
Right then I knew you cared.
Ooo Fr. Jim
Ooo Fr. Jim

Of course, being sarcastic collegians, they had to add the line, "Father Jim is paying us. That's why we wrote this hymn." The lyrics also made me wonder which freshman party I missed. I might have chosen to show how much I cared by busting it and assigning the perpetrators to trash detail.

When I was navigating the late 1970s in Alumni Hall, the legendary and still rectoring three decades later, Father George, was just a novice, ten years younger than I am now. He normally didn't appear until 2:00 PM which could be mostly excused by our knowledge that he stayed up until sunrise most nights, although it didn't prevent us from cracking vampire jokes about him.

Now I realize there is sometimes a method to a rector's apparent madness. We frequently laughed at Father George's obsession with cleanliness and order. He regularly prowled hallways until 3:00 or 4:00 AM with a small can of yellow paint and skinny artist's brush, painting over nicks we had kicked, punched, and scratched into the hallway corridors. Today's Dawgs are proud of the same diligent attention given to the hall's chapel which now has cushioned seats, fine altar fabrics, and parquet floors. Its surfaces are hand-waxed regularly. If you didn't have to wade through the fumes of sweaty hockey pads to get there, you would think you had wandered into Queen Elizabeth II's private chapel at Windsor Castle.

It took years for me to realize that doing crossword puzzles on a porch is a good way of picking up interesting tidbits. So too did lingering in hallways and pretending to be oblivious allow Father George to pick up the latest headlines from barking Dawgs carrying on with late-night bull sessions in their rooms. It also stops drunks from punching holes in walls if you're stalking the corridors later than they are. I must confess, however, that I do not share Father George's legendary endurance; the late-night inebriated usually outlast me, if not always the younger members of my staff.

My students sometimes stare at me quizzically and ask, "How did you know about that?" A rector needn't be a genius, just use of most of the five senses. Most times, we don't even have to leave our rooms. It helps to have the women's bathroom right across the hall from your own door so you can listen to the constant flow of information from unwitting messengers.

There is a general consensus among those who survived that being a rector in the 1970s meant spending weekend nights feeling like a riot policeman trying to control a liquored up World Cup crowd torching cars after the match. Our next door neighbors in Dillon Hall were widely known as the premier campus reprobates for their lewd songs, forced toga runs for freshmen, vandalism forays against neighboring halls, and something that went on with upperclassmen and a stuffed armadillo resting on a windowsill facing the South Quad that we in Alumni never fully understood.

The rector of Dillon in those years is now Bishop Daniel Jenky, C.S.C. of the Diocese of Peoria. In his first year as rector, the young C.S.C. priest tossed out thirty-six residents, about ten percent of the hall. To the rest of us observers, his headlong crusade against iniquity didn't seem to be making the barest dent in the hall's reputation, but we underestimated a rector's capacity to persevere over the long haul. Of course, some of his rector counterparts were lobbying for the legalization of kegs on campus on the spurious grounds that they made less mess than the leftover garbage heaps from forty cases of cheap beer hauled in by the trunkload at $4.99 each. But those moments of madness passed, and Notre Dame began gradually tightening up alcohol rules, as did college administrators across the country.

A few years later in 1984, the University unleashed a protest that flickered briefly into a raging storm. Notre Dame made national news when a couple of thousand undergraduates stormed the Golden Dome to protest a much more restrictive alcohol policy. Some alumni even rallied to their defense in the pages of the campus newspaper, *The Observer.* An angry mob headed toward Corby Hall calling for the committee chair's head on a platter. The chant of "We want beer!" was neither our students nor their handful of alumni supporters' finest hour.

It was the final gasp of the protest era, and University officials correctly determined that the threat of wholesale rebellion had largely petered out. That was the last time rectors seriously fretted about the God Quad going up in flames. Now we only feel like we are manning the drawbridge against a Vandal onslaught on Friday nights when there is daylong football pageantry scheduled for the next day.

When the future bishop lost a bet with his hall and agreed to allow residents to shave his beard off on the South Quad during lunch one day as payment, even the Alumni Dawgs put aside their feigned disinterest in their archrival's doings to see whether or not the Dillonites would cut his throat. The American episcopacy might have suffered greatly had he not been sharp enough to insist upon a professional barber to do the deed.

*   *   *   *

At times, it was infuriating and at others simply bewildering trying to pierce behind the foggy veil of misdirections that Father George used to keep his innermost thoughts from us. At one point when I was hall president, he asked, "Jim, do you think the hall government would contribute money to purchase a chandelier for the twenty-four hour lounge?" I was measured in my response. Like many administrators, I shifted the blame: "I don't think we have enough money in the budget for that. I doubt they will approve it," I said.

I didn't point out that we had plenty of spare change in the account to throw happy hours in the basement during football season. He urged me to think about it, but rarely does a hall president rally his supporters with offers of tasteful new lighting fixtures. I went to some friends and hooted about how ridiculous he was being. Eventually, Father George gave up on us and got his mother to donate it. After it came out of the crate, we thought it looked very nice, but we were glad we hadn't cut back on Hamms deliveries to fund it either.

Another time he asked me to fund a more expensive undertaking. "What would you think if we bought a glass display case and trophies for all the interhall sports?" He told me that he had priced a basketball trophy for $300 and a football one for $180 at a time when our annual hall tax used to fund activities was $10 per person. Between all the trophies he wanted to buy and the case, we were looking at a few grand.

"But Father, we haven't even won an interhall football or basketball championship that I know of. You want to spend that kind of money on trophies when we don't have anything to put on them?" I asked incredulously.

"Well," he said, "We'll win them *someday*." If I'd known he was working off a thirty year plan, I would have been more sympathetic. Instead I said, "I think it might be kind of dangerous to have a glass case in the middle of the hallway. Someone might fall into it and get hurt real bad. You know the way guys bump around and go crashing into walls." Funny, I'd never been concerned about that before, no more than our current crop worries about whether a side of scrambled eggs comes with their Solo cups on football Saturdays.

My objection only slowed him down momentarily. We won the interhall hockey championship later that year. Eventually, he would see the Dawgs win every other sport and engrave their triumphs happily on the hardware he succeeded in hornswaggling more visionary future presidents into funding. The glass stands today right where he wanted it, and it is windexed daily.

As far as I know, no mangy Dawg has ever plunged through the plate glass in his youthful exuberance. Among other lessons I learned from Father George and others like him, even if they took years to fully absorb, was that you don't win every battle right away. You just chip away little by little. It may take a few years, but eventually we get to the point where we can leave the drawbridges down at night without worrying about getting a spear in the chest.

Rectors, at least the male variety, are like army chaplains, immersed into a life that puts us shoulder to shoulder with 18 to 22 year olds who are oversexed and too often looking into a bottle for courage they have yet to develop within themselves. Sometimes we need to lecture or punish, but patience, humor, and gentle prodding are more delicate surgical instruments than thumping bibles. Sinners generally respond better when they are welcomed more than judged. Our strategy is the same essential principle taught at West Point about Grant during the Civil War. It's a war of attrition. We care most about the end result. We don't have to win every battle, just wear them down and outlast them.

*   *   *

My penultimate contest of wills began with Father George on a Sunday night in October of my sophomore year. I was sitting in my room studying when I noticed that the hallways seemed eerily quiet. Wondering why, I stood up and went to my door to look out. Nobody was around. Immediately, I heard the alleluia chant which precedes the gospel coming from the chapel and realized that I was the only one in my first floor section not at Mass.

I felt like I'd been knocked over by a linebacker. I was the only kid in grade school back at St. Gabe's who carried his own prayer book to and from church instead of following along with the paper missalettes provided in the pews, at least until third grade. Now after dreaming about attending Notre Dame since I was four, I was stunned to realize that I was the only one not going to church among my entire circle of friends.

But I was there the following week, posterior shifting uncomfortably on a wooden pew, and after that I did my imitation of the Energizer bunny. I just kept going and going. A few months later, Father George came up to me and said, "Jim, I think you should take charge of the hall choir." I laughed and said, "But Father I can't really sing all that well." I thought it was an iron-clad defense.

"Well, yes," he said, "but if you sing *everybody* else will want to sing too." I wasn't sure whether that rated as a compliment or not. But I dutifully rounded up a few others who sounded more like bellowing steers than opera tenors figuring that the more noise we made, the less anyone would be able to pick my voice out of the chorale. I never found the courage to solo, but a few years later I ended up in the seminary.

I am convinced that if I had not attended Notre Dame I would never have felt abandoned in a dorm corridor on a Sunday night and realized that I was not where I should have been. I also seriously doubt that I ever would have become a priest if Father George hadn't seen something in me that I didn't. It is not surprising that more Holy Cross priests have been ordained from his hall than any other since I first drove up Notre Dame Avenue.

Sometimes I think I would willingly take duty every weekend night for a year to get a look at the recommendation letter he wrote to the seminary's vocation director on my behalf. Priests aren't supposed to lie, but I'm mighty glad he fudged a few things. I've glossed over a few imperfections too when the forms come from bar associations asking me to attest to a former resident's moral character. We may keep that long rope on hand, but later we easily forget why we were tempted to use it.

We have many talented students, but that does not mean that they always perceive their own gifts clearly. One of our more important roles is to get them thinking about how to discern a vocation, not just a career – to think and pray about possibilities they had never imagined and realize that *how* one lives is at least as important as what one does. It can result in a small difference of perspective or a life-changing attitude.

There are many people teaching in classrooms, operating in hospitals, and sitting on benches in courtrooms because someone said, "I think you'd make a good (fill in the blank)" when it was the farthest thing from their own minds. There are also a couple occupying rector recliners until the wee hours of a Friday or Saturday evening at Notre Dame because someone saw a glimmer of promise that had previously gone undetected. I regularly vacation with one who recently finished up four years in the job. Eleven years ago, he was a student on my floor. I walked down to his RA room at 11:30 one night and out of the blue asked, "Have you ever thought of being a priest?" Father Dan will quickly admit that he might be running a construction firm in Portland, Oregon, today if I hadn't.

And so, a few years after I walked into an empty corridor, I ended up in the seminary. It will always be a mystery to some extent, but I find it deliciously ironic that I have not moved all that far in thirty years since. The highlight of my week is now standing behind the altar on Sunday nights and looking out at all of them for that one hour when they appear as the people they would, in the deep recesses of their hearts, truly desire to be.

I'm still walking around dorm corridors and, among other things, recruiting students to sing in the hall's Sunday Mass choir. I too now operate under the theory that it's a good idea to get a few froggy voices wailing up there to buck up others that it's alright to join in. Father George knew me better than I did myself, and he helped me get back to someplace I belonged – in a pew. It's only one of a rector's jobs, so I'm glad whenever I can assist people to match the lyrics in their soul with the tune they should be playing.

P.S., When I took charge of a hall for the first time as a young priest, my first thought was that it was disgustingly filthy. I immediately got some Brasso and started shining the doorplates. Now I keep the Sorin hallways relatively clean by shaming my RAs with a "dirtiest floor of the week" award at Sunday staff meetings.

P.P.S., Father George also conducted weekly bridge classes for us Dawgs, another thing I thought odd. He never got me to join in until twenty years later. Now he's my favorite – and most forgiving – partner.

P.P.P.S., We also have a glass trophy case in the Sorin hallway now. I'm just waiting for the Otters who have underachieved on the athletic fields during my tenure to win something to put it in.

CHAPTER 8

TENDER MERCIES

COLLEGE BOYS CRY TOO, and not just when they split a tibia during an interhall football game. Most tears I've seen have been shed by those few each year who break down while sitting on my couch, usually about something stupid or insignificant to anyone else except them. They bounce back from sporadic hangovers and sports injuries rather easily, but there are no honor badges for invisible hurts. Some are closer to possessing the bodies of men than the brains, and more synapses need to develop for patience, wisdom, and perspective to emerge.

Occasionally, rectors unleash a flood by calling them in for one of those unscheduled talks they try to avoid by walking in the opposite direction when they see us lumbering around the hallways. I am grateful for e-mail because it's nearly impossible to claim, "I didn't get your message." Sometimes the attitude we get in response to a word of advice in disciplinary meetings is feigned obedience, so I am usually surprised when a small dent unexpectedly unleashes a bleeding river of emotions.

I once heard our disciplinary meetings compared to the Spanish Inquisition. It is true that sentence is usually decided before testimony is heard. We do not have forensic evidence, lie detector tests, or many willing witnesses willing to put their hands on a bible and swear oaths. The standards for judgment are necessarily less than "beyond a reasonable doubt." We often have to rely upon eyewitness reports by hall staff, and we take them at their word. On the other hand, with minor infractions heard at that level, the range of penalties doesn't vary much more than $50 or a few hours of community service one way or another.

Besides, we can be swayed by a convincing argument, and I do have a weakness for mercy when explanations are accompanied by sloppy guy tears. But rectors mainly try drumming into thick-skulled undergraduate heads that the best way to get a break is to tell the whole truth and nothing but. If they do and we can grant a "reduced sentence" within the boundaries mandated by expectations of relative consistency, we will. It's supposed to be a pastoral model, not a rigid, bureaucratic one.

I used to sweat the details more, but I doubt it makes much difference how much fine money or community service hours a person gets assessed. The important principle is that they learn to be truthful, and that's why I try to reward honesty. Discipline is an educational tool, and in those moments of examination a residence hall should be an ethics laboratory in personal choice-making. If by graduation they understand the importance of maintaining one's integrity even if it costs them in the short-term, they will save themselves many problems later on when they confront thornier ethical dilemmas in the workplace.

At times, the flooding follows directly upon a bleary-eyed student a little unsteady on his feet being accompanied back to the hall by a campus police officer. That usually happens either after 1:00 AM or on a football Saturday afternoon when we decide to skip one of the lesser contests and rest at home, blessedly alone in our recliners and listening to the stadium roars from a distance, enjoying those few weekend hours that don't feel like a home invasion.

So, I tell whoever it is that it's alright, pat them on the back, and inform their parents when I get the upset call that, "He's a good kid, and this is a fender bender, not a train wreck." I promise to accompany them to their disciplinary meeting at the Office of Residence Life. Sometimes I get one of those hugs that are a little awkward and have to scrub dried salt marks off my shoulder later. I go to check on them just to make sure that they haven't cast themselves into a pit of despondency, but they tend to recover quickly.

Occasionally, I'll throw out a line like, "Bill Clinton smoked pot in college, and he got elected president. You just threw up on your roommate. You can still be a lawyer and even run for the Senate later if you want." Most rules and laws short of a felony can be broken by a collegian without permanent damage, which is fortunate because a fair number are.

*   *   *

One October night after a USC football game here, I was just about to close my door. Fall break was beginning, and many students had already left for home. As it was nearing midnight, my assistant rector, Bart, and a couple RAs pushed their way in, bringing three guys I'd never seen in tow. They were visiting friends of a freshman Otter, and I was told they had been smoking marijuana right outside in the courtyard, not fifty feet from my room.

People do light up here but rarely right outside our own doors. However, students when roadtripping to other colleges often feel that they have a mystical kind of immunity away from whatever bubble they normally inhabit. I try to warn the Otters that hometown buddies busting into town for a weekend of partying at Notre Dame are a tidal wave of danger rushing toward them. Rarely does the speech make a dent.

Upon first interrogation, the three proto-criminals told us they only had the one joint that they had bought at a non-existent gas station a mile away. We found out what room they were staying in and that their host was asleep upstairs. I sent them back up with the staff members and told them to collect their things. They returned to my room, and I made them empty their bags – nothing there but sweaty clothes. Then I said, "Now turn out all your pockets." Reluctantly, one reached into his jeans and pulled out a baggie full of weed.

After confiscating it, I suppose I should have called the cops and sent them to jail, but instead I simply turned to them and said, "In five minutes, I'm going to pick up that phone next to my chair, and I'm going to call the police. I'm telling them that three guys matching your description just left this hall heading toward the parking lot, so if I were you I'd get going." One of them stood up hesitantly, but it was apparent they were confused and didn't quite get it, so I shouted, "GO. NOW!" and they bolted, grabbed their bags, dashed out the door, and kept running. I had no intention of picking up the phone. I believed my own dazed Otter when he told me that none of them had ever done pot in high school, and he had no idea that his weekend guests had started. Lucky for him, the sheet marks on his face bolstered his story.

I hoped that scaring three freshmen for whom it hadn't become a habit might be all they needed to straighten out. If they wound up with their mug shots in the police blotter later, they had their chance. They will experiment with things they shouldn't, but generally I prefer not to see eighteen year olds get records. Most dumb college stuff turns out to be no more than that, and I have wished on more than one occasion that mine hadn't been caught. Sometimes it's better to handle a matter informally, and luckily for them, these three normally made mischief under someone else's roof, not mine. They could take their chances once they got back there if they chose, but hopefully, this violation of what I often refer to as "the stupidity principle" made them hesitate before cruising alleys in search of another nickel bag of pot.

However, I have never forgotten one who developed a major drug and alcohol habit despite multiple forms of counseling, punishments, pleadings, and interventions. He was a bright guy and deceptively sensitive. He would, on occasion, keep me up later than usual asking penetrating theological questions. There are few students I've enjoyed word-sparring with as much. I

119

think he was daring God to prove Himself by rescuing him, but he pushed the envelope of dangerous living and tumbled into despair. He later made a half-hearted attempt at suicide, and it was chilling to see him drugged up at the psych ward walking down the corridor like a Frankenstein creature. He was still on psychotropic meds a few weeks later when I sat across from him in a university conference room for his suspension hearing. I knew we had to send him away, but I took it as a personal defeat.

I never saw him again, but he tracked me down and sent an e-mail message out of the blue after more than five years had passed. He had straightened himself out and was belatedly finishing college in another state. He thanked me for trying to help him. It's the kind of note that makes all of the short-term head-butting worthwhile. I wrote back but didn't get a second response. I let him go because I suspected that further contact would have been awkward for him, but sometimes I pause to wonder if he's still OK.

*   *   *

One year the first week of the semester had passed with little trouble. I went up to an RA's room on the following Saturday night to see how things were ending after one of our larger rooms had sponsored a small social gathering. I was standing about four feet inside the door chatting casually a little after 1:30 AM. with two staff members seated on a couch. A couple more students came by, standing between me and door. Then a very exuberant freshman came and stood in the entrance.

"I am so f----g wasted. This is just f----g great. I love college.

I just had the best f-----g time ever." He should have been able to see me from where he was standing. Perhaps he was confused about why four student witnesses were doubling over in laughter, but he plowed ahead along the same lines with similar vocabulary before running out of breath while still staring directly at me.

One of the RAs turned to him and said, "Jimmy, how would you like to meet your rector?"

Jimmy came over and shook my hand and said, "Hey, how are you doing?"

"Very well," I said nonchalantly. "How about you?"

"Great!" he shouted. Then he turned, walked away. The crowd howled even louder. I peered out into the corridor; he was walking straight. I couldn't quite figure it out.

The next day about noon, I ran into another priest-rector who has much darker hair, is fifteen years older, and six inches taller than I. Rev. Paul Doyle, C.S.C, who's been watching over Dillon Hall for more than a decade, came up to me and said in his Virginia drawl, "I don't know who thuh baw was or what he did last night, but one of yaws just came boundin' down yaw steps thah'uh in Sorin apolawgizin' for whatevah it was."

I gave a description of Jimmy and asked if it was him. Father Doyle said, "That's the baw." The only rational explanation I could imagine for why Jimmy failed to identify me and then confused me with a lanky Virginia gentleman ten hours later was that he didn't have his contacts in. I decided not to inquire further. I waited a year and a half before asking, and it turned I'd been right about his vision problem. He'd had a few brewskies but not as many as I'd feared. Interestingly, I never heard him swear like that again, and he became one of our regular daily communicants soon thereafter. Score one for the "Don't beat them over the head if they don't really need it" philosophy of education.

Similarly, one Friday night on a football weekend, another first semester freshman was in the midst of a loud potty mouth phase, dropping f-bombs that could be heard a floor away. He was gushing forth like a city fire hydrant in summer oblivious that his father was turning the hallway with his nine-year-old sister about fifteen feet behind him. I usually appreciate it when parents arrive early for their periodic visits.

Perhaps he has too, but neither can I recall hearing him toss another verbal grenade like that since. I'm proud of both for that hint of growth and many other signs of goodness and generosity they have displayed in the years since. Most don't get such a mortifying lesson, and are not so inclined to follow the urgings of their local priest in the absence of one. However, I am always glad when my raised eyebrow shaming techniques about their language, as with the revealing poster girls on their walls, receive a booster rocket of support from some other source.

The next year I was driving up the hill out back on a Thursday night to return a car to Corby Hall when I saw a group of twelve or so coming out the southwest door next to the Quint. It initially appeared like they were heading out to cheerfully greet a hallmate. I briefly considered rolling down my window to be friendly too and say hi as I was swinging around the corner. They were so preoccupied they didn't see me driving up two cars back behind the vehicle that had their attention.

I circled around to the front of Corby about fifty yards away and glanced back. I thought I saw the group hurriedly carting in some square boxes, all of the same size from a car's trunk, though at that distance I couldn't be as certain as I'd need to be if I were called into a witness box by a county prosecutor. By the time I got out of my car, they had all scurried rat-like back into the hall.

I had to drop off the car keys and pick up my mail, but when I got back to Sorin, I hung out by the room where I suspected the goods had landed for a couple of minutes until one of the residents came out. Coincidentally, he was carrying a permission form for a social gathering he and his roommates wanted to hold the following night. I asked him, "Which of you has a four-door cream sedan with license plate number BAD 123?"

"That's David," he said.

"Well, just a suggestion," I responded. "Next time you bring twelve people out to unload, you might want to make sure there aren't headlights coming up the driveway, and one set doesn't belong to your rector – just a suggestion. Oh, and you might want to make sure you don't get an early start tonight," I added. An hour later I saw him and some of his roommates heading out to play hoops which seemed like a fair resolution since they were sometimes inclined to start the weekend early. I was pleased. No blood spilled. Quid pro quo. Sometimes it pays to negotiate.

Still, rectors inevitably struggle with being consistent. Students will pillory those who aren't, though their exacting measurement standards rarely discourage them from seeking an exception in their own self-interest. At a certain point, you just get worn down saying no continually and cave in to someone with a story that sounds like they really are a victim of circumstances beyond their control.

A hall full of male college students isn't much different than a football team. They don't like discipline, but they perform better with it. The first reaction of most would be to say that they would prefer not to have rules, but an honest one will tell you that he likes it better when they are enforced squarely. They also believe, with some merit, that a good kid doesn't normally deserve to get shafted for getting unlucky once. On the other hand, the chronic offenders who regularly cause trouble but somehow manage to elude detection don't deserve a whole lot of breaks when they finally slip up. Aside from consistency and patience, I've already alluded to the other key to being a decent rector: the ability to discriminate between a small battle and one worth fighting.

*   *   *

When I was a second-year seminarian, a bunch of us got into a dither about something silly. Our superior had prohibited us, along with the cooks and maintenance staff, from having a dollar-a-square football pool because some of our classmates with a bad case of excessive piety had convinced him that gambling of any kind was immoral and inappropriate. A seminary world can be even smaller than a dorm, and there was a major to-do. I remember at one point writing a three-page, single-spaced manifesto of outrage that I hope nobody ever finds buried in a file drawer.

At the end of the following year, I was officially meeting with Rev. John Gerber, C.S.C. for the last time as a seminarian. I am embarrassed to admit there were times we hadn't gone easy on him and had behaved not much better than undergraduates. At the end of that one-on-one, he jumped up from his chair, stuck out his hand toward me, and graciously said, "Jim, I just want you to know how much I've enjoyed tussling with you."

Father John had a knack for using SAT words that were not part of most people's regular vocabulary, as one might expect from a former English literature professor. There have been several occasions since when I have told that story to a group of students in an opening year address or in a homily. I want them to understand that whatever bruises we inflict upon one another are easily forgotten, like the kind we get from playing tackle snow football on the quad.

There are serious situations, and occasionally, I've gone nuclear, with justification and irrationally without, but I do enjoy the everyday give and take. I hope they realize it later if not in a heated room, and I'm grateful that Father John showed me how to put tussles behind me. He may have been a seminary rector, but I keep his picture on my desk to remind me of what a priest should be, wherever he puts on his black shirt.

It took me a while to learn a few things though. As a young

rector, the first student I ever gave community service hours fell victim to the fact that I heard him and a couple of his friends talking loudly with the door closed after quiet hours as I was passing by. If I had been ten feet away, I wouldn't have heard them at all. After he completed one hour of community service cleaning in the basement, I let him go because I realized quickly how knee-jerk I'd been. He went on to become of the better hall presidents and RAs I ever had. Now, I just bark at them to shut up and turn the stereo or karaoke machine off at 2:00 AM when I hear it from a hundred feet away on weekend nights, unless they are habitual offenders or the music is signaling some other problem.

I used to think that my top priority was to establish control and authority over them, but that was the attitude of a neophyte, beset with fear and insecurity much like a first year teacher. Sometimes a rector inherits a tough situation and has to do some remedial work to clean up a mess another left behind, but the most vital thing is simply to let them know you care about them and show it by being around more than not. It's a far better way of garnering their respect – and compliance. I've been fortunate to have mentors wiser than I who have at times corrected my wrongful impulses.

As much as I enjoy watching them navigate the inevitable hurdles, achieve leadership positions, and receive their diplomas on Commencement Sunday, I relish even more the opportunities to preside at their marriages and baptize their children – especially the ones that I have tussled mightily with. But I regret the ones I never really knew. Sometimes it's a deficit of chemistry. We pass in the corridor or on the quad day after day and never do much more than exchange names, but other times I know that I could have exerted a little more energy and cared more than I did.

CHAPTER 9

A Day in Our Life

OVER THE LAST ELEVEN YEARS since I returned to Notre Dame, I've crossed paths with Rhodes Scholarship winners and multiple undergrads who graduated with perfect 4.0's. I helped one develop an idea for a valedictory speech that was the best I've heard, although I might be a wee bit biased. I've known many who have gone on to Ivy League law and medical schools or other premier graduate programs. There are piles of recommendation letters on my hard drive for people who deserve most of the superlatives I write on their behalf, especially once they've reached senior year and worked out the behavioral kinks from their freshmen and sophomore escapades. I am even more impressed by the ones with the steady work ethics whom I see in the study lounge every day plugging away, struggling to stay close to a 3.0 GPA in chemical engineering.

But every once in a while I'm tempted to ask one who's fairly close to the mean, academically and behaviorally, to give a speech to parents in August, describing a normal day just to register their reactions, something like:

I usually get up at ten after five or six hours sleep. If I haven't done laundry in three or four weeks, I just dig something out of the pile that I sprayed with Fabreze a couple of days earlier. If I've run out of deodorant, I'll squirt a little under my arms too (I'm not making that up).

It's partly cloudy and thirty degrees outside so no reason not to wear shorts and flip flops to class. I'll just throw on my Sorin sweatshirt. I might as well bring my laptop and save some time by doing e-mail or surfing the Net during class since the prof's PowerPoint slides are all posted on his web space anyway.

I rarely eat breakfast except when my parents come to town and wake me up early, so I'll go to lunch, eat a beef sandwich, a couple of tacos, a pile of french fries, and a half a plate of spaghetti before deciding on what to have for seconds, if I'm hungry. I'll pass by the fruit but grab a couple of cookies and make a foot-high, soft-serve chocolate ice cream cone for myself on the way out. I'll pick up a copy of today's Observer and maybe do the crossword puzzle to kill some time. After that, I only have about two hours until my next class, so I might do a little reading.

Then I'll go to my second class and likely fall asleep, but it's a lecture with a hundred people, so no one will notice. After I come back, I suppose I'll go throw a football around on the quad. By that time, it's 4:00 or so, and if I haven't thought about what I'm going to do this weekend, I'll log into Facebook to see who's having a party and update my posting with some pictures from the bash down on Madison Street last weekend.

It's dinner time already, and I have a meeting afterward at LaFun (LaFortune Student Center) about a coed Twister game on the quad that I'm supposed to be helping out with on Sunday. Then, I have to meet with my business class project group because we have a twenty-page report that's due at the end of the week, and I haven't started writing my part yet. By the time I get back, it's 9:30, and I'm heading off for hoops at 10:30, so I might as well watch some TV. After I get back at midnight, I suppose I should do take a look at my history notes because I have a test in a couple of days, and I've gotten behind. I'm just too busy. All this work is stressing me out.

It may not sound much different than their parents' college experiences in days of old except that a lot of our students are keeping time like this and still making the dean's list. Also, more of them are staying up until 3:00 or 4:00 rather than 1:00 or 2:00 AM as we typically did. The smarter yet sleep-deprived generation can skate by doing less studying than their folks, but with grade inflation, still get admitted to a darn good law school. It's a tougher grind for the pre-meds and engineers. Since they can't fake their way through calculus equations or chemistry formulas, they are generally motivated to use their spare hours more wisely.

While I know firsthand that constant griping wears anyone down, professors cave in too easily rather than standing up to kids who come in to bargain about grades. The neurotic ones think they are being oppressed whenever a little minus sign appears next to their 'A.' I had to get a 3.4 to make the dean's list. Today, it is over 3.7 in Arts and Letters. They may be inherently smarter than I was, but rampant grade inflation devalues the records of students with 3.9 GPAs who really do cherish their educations, are interested in going on for a Ph.D., and read whole books instead of cliff notes.

I know it's important to have time for research, but I do wish more of our profs would teach on Fridays, so the undergraduate's typical four-day work week doesn't turn into a three-day weekend. That only encourages them to blow off until Sunday afternoon when they pick up the books for a twelve-hour burst to compensate for dallying the previous two days. I'm not surprised when they show up for Monday morning classes groggier than they were on Thursday.

They have shorter weeks but longer days. Classes after 5:30 PM used to be rarities but not anymore. Evening courses are fine for graduate students, but between classes, band or choir practice, resume-building meetings for organizations, student government meetings, clubs, or other events peppered more widely throughout the day, many undergrads don't finally arrive home until their professors are in bed. Ideally, they would be more disciplined in their use of those one- or two-hour gaps between classes that are now more prevalent since the work day has stretched out into the evening, but many of the younger ones are still at a stage where they need help managing time.

I never schedule a meeting in the hall before 10:30 PM because it is impossible to bring an entire group together any earlier. Rectors and students alike are becoming increasingly nocturnal creatures, like the giant raccoons and opossums invading the campus. The sheer volume of activities, programs, organizations, student employment, workshops, research positions, presentations, and lectures being promoted to students with little coordination among departments is overwhelming.

If we simply divided the campus population into the quantity of opportunities being pushed, we would probably discover that we are churning out two to three times more unsustainable programming to a student body that has only grown incrementally each year since I arrived. I'd like to see a consulting firm come in to audit the amount of activity we are generating to test my hypothesis.

I've heard some complaints from professors that it's not unusual to have only a handful of students show up for a lecture from four-star quality guest speakers. Some of our students may be anti-intellectual. It is true that fewer of them go on for Ph.Ds than at comparable institutions. With one-third of our upperclassmen pursuing a business degree, it is obvious that too many look at a Notre Dame degree primarily as a meal ticket to a six- or seven-figure salary.

Still, we could do better at structuring our weeks and eliminating superfluous programs so that others with more motivation to expand their intellects wouldn't be required to make as many Hobbesian choices. The walls of my building are virtually wallpapered sometimes two and three deep on bulletin boards with oversized (and expensive) color posters that go mostly unnoticed simply because there are so many of them.

*   *   *

Student services departments have become professionalized and expanded greatly because universities' legal liability has increased so dramatically within the last generation. We are long past the days where students can organize a slip 'n slide on the quad without signing legal waivers and filling out multiple forms mandated by risk management officers. The common wisdom used to be that the secretaries really ran the place, but now it's IT people and lawyers. We're more afraid of lawsuits even though our endowment made a twenty-five perecent return last year of $1.5 billion. Logically, the wealthier we are, the less we should worry.

It's part of the state of nature that late adolescents are particularly prone to rebel instinctively against our efforts to keep them safe. Every time we come up with new security systems, whether by installing door alarms or substituting ID cards for keys, our students are adept at finding ways to thwart them. They are so trusting about their immunity from harm, I wouldn't be surprised to see one let in Osama bin Laden if he knocked at the front door and asked to use the bathroom.

Maybe it's too much to expect one place to stand against a culture of fear that lurks like a riptide underneath our daily routines. The reasonable standard no longer applies. We are supposed to be telepathic about the intentions of twisted loners' minds at the same time that our campus counselors are legally prevented from sharing information about them. No one wants to be the lead story on Fox News.

An even bigger frustration is that we used to have a familial culture here, but it is gradually being transformed into one that is corporate, bureaucratic, and balkanized. Even though the student body is only seventeen percent larger than thirty years ago, we have tripled the number of staff employed here since. In the

'70s, I could walk down the hallways of a classroom building and see one or at most two office assistants in a department, know them by sight and often by name. It was fairly easy to figure out which human being I had to speak with to get an answer to some minor question. When alumni walk around marveling at the new campus construction, they have little idea that the multiplication of offices inside has transformed daily life even more. It is one more example of progress' double-edged, unintended consequences.

We recently spent more than $40 million on upgrading hardware and software with the goal of becoming more technologically advanced, paperless, and efficient. However, I would be hard-pressed to find a department that within the last few years hasn't churned out more paper. We needed to get beyond the mentality of a mom and pop store operating out of a cookie jar, but we are no longer a lean organization in which a phone call and a little common sense can necessarily fix a small problem.

It took five years to get my address correct in the telephone directory because my information defied the logic of preexisting database categories. My administrative assistant, who probably spent fifty hours over those years trying to sort it out, was actually told by a staffer at one point, "Your building doesn't exist."

One rector recently told me he was still trying to get a student's ID card working five weeks after the beginning of the academic year. The glitch was still getting passed like a pinball between three different departments. The consequence of spending hours to accomplish what should be simple tasks has rectors these days lamenting that they are doing more motel management than ministry. There are days when I feel like a dazed wanderer in a Kafka novel and wonder whether it would be easier to deal with the Social Security Administration or an airline customer service center.

*   *   *

I suspect that whatever time we have saved becoming more technologically efficient has been roughly offset by the amount we spend dealing with computer glitches and corresponding on e-mail. I receive thirty to forty e-mails on a slow day. I immediately delete the outside spam, but I am also reflexively dumping most departments' priority messages into the same electronic trash bin without a second thought.

There is barely a day that goes by when I don't get an e-mail from someone I don't know asking me to recruit students for their organization, event, or program. Unless it's something I care about personally, I just hit "delete." My general coping mechanism is not to respond to mass mailings from University employees I've never heard of just because they show up on my computer instead of as paper in my regular mailbox.

E-mailing is not an effective means of communication between strangers when it isn't personal. It's just more junk mail that we use as a crutch when human contact would be more effective. It might take more time to make the rounds of offices regularly and chat a bit, but over the long haul hoofing it around the beat makes more friends. They come in handy when a person really needs a favor. We don't hear as much these days about

136

the virtues of MBWA, management by walking around. I asked a business professor recently whether he thought it had been rendered obsolete by e-mail. He assured me that the professional literature on management problems in wired workplaces is quickly expanding.

I don't think I'm a Luddite despairing of all forms of progress, but occasionally I do think we'd be better off if neither e-mail nor the Internet had ever been invented. In the last century we became different people when light pollution effectively blotted out the stars in the evening sky. We ceased gazing in awe at the heavens that humble us into acknowledging that we may not be the universe's focal point.

In this one, we are better networked but growing increasingly impersonal, imitating our students who spend more time gazing at computer screens and less talking to one another, except on cell phones. Inter-office communication between employees at Notre Dame can go on for years without face-to-face contact or even a human voice at the other end of a phone line. We are text messaging more but growing farther apart.

The wider chasm between academic and residential life makes it more challenging to maintain a sense of common mission when we rarely interact across divisions. Rectors have difficulty grasping why professors are so preoccupied with publishing articles. Profs have little idea how much rectors get worn down dealing with the demands of a hundred times more kids living under our roofs than they have running around beneath theirs at home. Even in the small world of Notre Dame, there are hundreds of orbits that can lurch from one day to the next without intersecting except over fiber optic wire.

This year I started trying to elevate my Otters' minds by using University funding to subsidize their attendance at cultural events in our new DeBartolo Performing Arts Center. The opportunity to watch a regular stream of ballets, concerts, plays, and foreign cinema in a state-of-the-art facility has begun to transform the cultural life of campus within just a few years. I am glad to encourage more of them to avail themselves of those offerings. I just don't know what kind of bribery I can offer that will effectively result in greater attendance at free evening lectures or expand their interest in doing research, particularly when we are pushing so much superfluous programming though I have started paying for lunches with professors in the hope that it might spark some intellectual germ to life.

This year I also started an "Otter of the Week" award. There is no prize money, just an e-mail message (I guess I'm guilty of cluttering inboxes too!) highlighting the lesser known accomplishments of our residents whether those be for distinction in campus ministry or service activities, cultural performances, or academic accomplishments. Over the long haul, I hope that bombarding them with concrete examples of good peer role models being productive will encourage more to think along similar lines.

The University has initiated programs to arrange dinners between professors and students, and I suspect those on the academic side would welcome more opportunities to mingle and talk about their research. In the spring of 2007, the University's president, Rev. John Jenkins, C.S.C. opened up a campus-wide inquiry about several areas of importance, including how to work more effectively across divisions and "create a culture of service excellence to support the University's mission."

I was thrilled to see the announcement. I hope it helps. It's hard to figure out how to encourage better communication when everyone seems to be: a) too busy doing meaningful work; b) pretending to be busier than they are; or c) busy circulating paper and e-mail messages that barely anyone else reads. I'm tired about asking people how they're doing and hearing, "I'm really busy." I'd like to hear someone respond just once, "I'm really productive."

*   *   *

However, it is not just the gap between University divisions but the widening distance among the students within our own halls that bothers me. More of them live today behind closed doors. In Alumni Hall, we used to gather in the hallways in the evenings and shoot the bull with one another for an hour or two. We could only get four snowy stations on our thirteen inch black and white TVs and had to go to a bowling alley or arcade to play a video game. Talking was our main form of nightly entertainment, and the practice helped us learn how to narrate a good story. A casual observer would conclude that today's students spend more time yakking much more inanely with friends on cell phones glued to their ears than speaking face-to-face. I regularly hear one side of the conversations.

"Yo."

"What's up?"

"I dunno."

"Tonight, not sure yet."

"Really."

"Did he?"

"Well, maybe."

"Yeah, later."

End of conversation. Yakking constantly about nothing.

In some halls, a staff member can walk down the hallways at midnight and rarely run into a student during what is prime-time for them. Our undergraduate's heads are turned to their laptops more than their neighbors down the hall, looking up lecture notes, playing video games, instant messengering, doing Internet research, surfing porn sites, gambling online, and reviewing Facebook profiles. It got worse last year when we succumbed to the pressure of many years and finally installed cable in every residence hall room. I have begun to worry almost as much about what they are doing alone over the Internet on weekdays as what they are doing with one another off-campus on weekends.

It is the curse of our times that we can engage in instant communication with people all over the globe, but we take less time to know the people with whom we live and work side by side. It isn't just the wider world that is growing smaller. Too many of us are becoming like dwarf stars, collapsing our identities into a computer screen, walking around with laptops that function as surrogate friends. We may not be free to ignore the Information Age, but I wish that professors would ban laptops from classrooms where they are not absolutely necessary and stop putting their PowerPoints online. It only enables lazy students who waste their parents' tuition money IMing when they should be taking notes in class.

Cutting off their e-mail and Internet access after midnight might not be such a bad idea either. Those of us who are employed here should draw up some guidelines limiting our e-mail use too. Even if we didn't want to leave our desks, we would know one another better if we would use the telephone more often and match a voice to a net ID name. I know most modern organizations have similar issues. We cannot avoid the progress that has made us a virtual community, but we need to know one another better to be a more virtuous one.

CHAPTER 10

THEY DO KNOW
HOW TO PRAY

Working on my theology degree twenty years ago, I never imagined that I would live to see several hundred students marching in a Eucharistic Procession at Notre Dame and celebrating Benediction on the front steps of the Dome. After the reforms of Vatican II, those devotions virtually disappeared from the Catholic landscape along with May Crownings. Nevertheless, a few years ago, the procession made a comeback here, following several years of requests from students for more adoration of the Blessed Sacrament.

Many Vatican II products, a generation or two older than I, thought that the Council was a definitive turning point in Church history and its reforms would prove normative for all future times. They never imagined that millions of young people would cheer a Polish Pope like a football hero for advocating a culture of life and calling them to reinvigorate centuries-old practices thought to be passé. Today, some remain puzzled by seemingly normal seminarians wearing the cassocks they pitched into trash cans and label too readily as "conservative" those students whose piety is more traditional.

But every generation rebels in some form against the last. The revolutionaries of one era become the establishment figures of the next. So many theological and political idealists have wrongly imagined that the banners they waived in their youth marked a definitive break with the past. The last century heard the end of history proclaimed, listened to reassurances from diplomats that war was had been rendered obsolete by technology, and even read books by people purporting to be theologians that "God is dead." God and war are very much still with us, and both history and religion go through cycles, if erratically.

I believe that young people are generally idealists masquerading as cynics, outwardly afraid to defy convention while yearning inwardly for the courage to do so. Many stroll around in A & F or Aeropostale t-shirts, but a fair number of ours sport ones that advertise their attendance at World Youth Day as well. One constant is that young people proclaim what they believe not only by what they do but by what they wear. Those with a more religious bent feel a need to publicly counteract the more trivial and degrading messages of a trashy society. If some of their peers want to put multiple spikes through their lips and nipples – or worse – the believers also want to cry out that not everyone under the age of twenty-one accepts those extreme displays as conventional or healthy.

There are Catholic reactionaries of all ages scattered across the country, including seminarians who don robes because religious garb confers a superficial aura of authority upon those who are inwardly insecure. There is even a handful of students on our campus who act like Inquisition informants, closely scrutinizing priests to insure they don't make the slightest changes in the wording of Mass parts and writing our local bishop whenever they spot an imaginary act of "heresy."

That kind of behavior partially reflects the judgmental tendencies of young people who are much quicker to demand perfection from adults than to examine their own inconsistencies. In older people, it signifies a brittle ideological narrowness or lack of proportion, the inability to distinguish, in more generic terms, between a trivial issue and a vital one. There are many levels of nuance in Church teaching between detailed rubrics and our creedal belief that Jesus rose from the dead. We should all remember that rigid people who impose modern variations of pharisaical legalism upon others are mirroring the same attitudes that He consistently decried among His own people.

Nevertheless, there are also those young people on campuses, in seminaries, and in convents today who are simply and normally religious. A surprising number defy traditional categories by embracing the "liberal" social teaching of the Church but adopting "conservative" stances on life issues and devotional practices. They aren't freaks or ideologues but healthy people unafraid to let others know that they wish to be followers of Christ. They intuitively grasp better than their elders that living as a sacramental Church in a visually-oriented culture requires Christians to be walking signs of faith.

My generation was trained in the seminary to avoid any semblance of clericalism even to the point of putting on suits and ties to teach theology classes. But today, a priest is more likely to be rebuked than to receive deference for wearing a collar down the street. I occasionally wonder whether we should intentionally put on black for shopping trips to the mall as a sign of our willingness to do penance for our brothers' sins against youth?

Our students like to see us in uniform because it gives them permission to display their own faith more informally in public. It is ironic that a black shirt can be a simultaneously a sign of penance and one of fidelity, but aren't we all sinners and disciples simultaneously? It's one thing we have in common with our students, and it is altogether appropriate that we be willing to display how we are both like and unlike them but with humility instead of arrogance. There is a middle ground somewhere even if the spectrum itself shifts over time.

*   *   *

In my second year in Sorin, I decided to initiate a yearly retreat. I was aiming for twenty people and wasn't sure it was would fly, so I tapped nine popular leader types for the team. One thing I learned back as a sophomore in Alumni Hall was that ninety-five percent of the time, people follow people more than signs and posters. If you want to draw a crowd, get the names of pack leaders on the signup sheet before waving it in front of other Dawgs – or Otters.

We were holding our first planning meeting late on a Tuesday night. As soon as I mentioned prayer, the first comment was, "We don't want this to get too religious or anything, or it will just turn people off." There is still a bell curve, if a flatter one – more overtly religious ones and more bingeing partygoers at both ends but most still somewhere in the middle. They are content to express their faith through Mass attendance and private prayer but need encouragement to share their thoughts publicly. Nevertheless, on the retreat, despite a singular dislike for "sharing" or forced group discussions, some of those kids did come out with the darndest things. Then ten seconds after the session closed, they jumped up to play poker and tuned into a basketball game.

Two years is the college equivalent of a chemical half-life. Anything lasting that long is a certifiable tradition sacred as the alma mater after a football game. Now I no longer worry about imposing too much religion. For the third annual retreat, I simply told the team we would have two prayer sessions and three talks on faith, service, and commitment. I informed them that for the first planning meeting they would each share a story of faith that was personally transformative.

At the end of it, I told them, "I would close this with a prayer, but the last hour has been a prayer. You were all quite eloquent and showed that you can speak personally and profoundly without a note in front of you. This is what we are going to do and get the others to do on the retreat." I did make one change after the first year. I found a place out in the woods that didn't have a TV. I still brought steaks, cards, and footballs, but, sufficiently prepped, they brought a capacity for honest conversation that defies stereotypes about college males' willingness to speak personally in small groups of peers.

*   *   *

Notre Dame's Campus Ministry sponsors about fifty of their

own retreats each year. By the time they graduate, a good share of our undergraduates attend at least one, and while it is a long way from the days of compulsory church attendance, most estimates of Sunday undergraduate participation hover somewhere around fifty to sixty percent Some go to the Basilica on Sunday morning, though even the 11:45 AM Folk Choir Mass is early for most.

The overwhelming majority don't go to "church" but to chapels, located in every residence hall, the graduate apartment complex, the Law School lounge, plus occasional Masses for retreat groups, Hispanics, and class gatherings at the Grotto. Most hall Masses start at 10:00 PM. and end at the same hour that their alumni grandfathers would have been commanded to put lights out. Freed from mandatory edicts, most Catholic students – and a fair number who aren't – opt to show up on Sunday anyway. Outside of the Third World, Notre Dame is one of the few places on the planet where a significant share show up without shoes. It may be just about the only way Domers resemble most people their age in Bangladesh or Uganda, but the key point is that they come because at most other Catholic colleges and universities, they don't.

Generally, institutions of higher learning attempt to keep students close to campus believing the more they do, the more they will bond with the place – and become loyal alumni donors later on. It is clear to me after nearly two decades of observation in Notre Dame residence halls, those who remain on campus all four years do attend Mass at a higher rate than the ones who move off their junior or senior year. It would be an interesting study to correlate undergraduate attendance with giving patterns later, but I wouldn't want the results to become the basis for a marketing plan to boost Mass crowds either.

The celebration of Sunday Eucharist is so important to hall life that most rectors consider attendance to be a job requirement for RAs, even those of other faiths. We aren't proselytizing, but it is the central event of the weekend, even in the fall once the stadium crowds have stopped tailgating. It is probably a good thing that we don't get too many outside wanderers on Sunday nights, aside from an occasional parent, sibling, or high school friend visiting.

The post-Mass announcements, particularly in the men's halls, show how quickly they can shift gears. From a reverent post-communion silence, the atmosphere moves quickly after the closing prayer to something like an open session at the mike in a comedy club. The one who likes to remind me to "Be good" launched a campaign to raise money for Haitians and concluded the Sorin announcements each week with a "Haitian fun fact" like: "I almost got fired from Subway today because a guy got mad at me for trying to convince him to use mayo instead of dressing on his sub."

I know it has nothing to do with Haiti; I don't get it; and I can't figure out why anyone laughs. I'm not surprised that he's barely raised $100 in two years, but he does get a lot of attention. He got mine his freshman year when he started calling me "Kingpin," but I kind of like that. I figure one good turn deserves another, so I usually greet our hall president by shouting, "Hail Caesar!"

Outside observers might also be scandalized by the bare feet and "Muck Fichigan" t-shirts that some don't bother to change before waltzing into the chapel. I selectively comment on their outerwear to make them reflect a bit upon the conflict between the words they wear with the Word they hear, particularly when it coincides with a lecture from St. Paul about modest dress. Perhaps they are confused by my relative leniency toward their shirt sales operations outside the chapel. I admit to drawing crooked lines sometimes about how much propriety to demand of them.

The incongruities of expression during Mass time are heightened by the spontaneous prayers of petition which slice through the congregation poignantly when we open it up to them: "For my grandmother who died this afternoon;" "For a high school friend who committed suicide yesterday and for his family;" "For my father who is having open-heart surgery tomorrow;" "For a friend from home who was paralyzed in a car accident."

Often they will not have said a word to me, yet they are moved to utter their anxieties and sorrows aloud in front of a hundred people. Even the well-rounded ones experience moments of fragility, and underneath the surface bravado lurk insecurities and fears, just like the rest of us. I am glad that our students have chapels down the hall where they can go to relieve their burdens. Often when I hear what they didn't want to tell me in person, they are relieved when I follow up to inquire.

Rev. John O'Hara, C.S.C., who was a one-man Campus Ministry in the 1920s before becoming University president and later

Cardinal Archbishop of Philadelphia, had an office next door to my room which is now Father Malloy's residence. There used to be a sliding door between that and the rear wall of the chapel. When a person wanted to go to confession, he would knock on it; Father O'Hara would put on his stole and take a seat. Today, they just tap on my door. It's a good thing there was always a screen when Coolidge was president. Father O'Hara would have been aghast at their t-shirts, but I doubt what he heard differed much from what I listen to in my room or in one of the confessionals at the Basilica.

My last year in the seminary we had a class on how to hear confessions, but there is nothing that can prepare a priest for the humility of the sacrament. When first ordained, I was scrupulous about trying to match a penance appropriate to the sin. However, I have found that most people's sins are fairly similar and ordinarily human, yet the most innocuous can walk in feeling like the proverbial ax murderer.

Now I think the point is usually to persuade penitents to let go of the ball and chain they are dragging around. My favorite penance is to ask them to take a full inventory of everything they have done right since their last confession. In most cases, people should walk out of the confessional feeling liberated, realizing they are mostly good people who do a few things wrong, not awful ones branded with doom.

Father O'Hara would also be surprised no doubt by the handholding at the Our Father and hugging at the Sign of Peace. I'm not a huggy guy, but the tendency has grown in the last few years since I arrived in Sorin. The Sorin hug used to be a grappler's sturdy handshake followed by a thumping chest butt, but the full open-armed embrace has been gaining in popularity. Since more football players do it these days after a touchdown, maybe we shouldn't be surprised to find life mirroring TV. Sometimes the hugging lasts longer than communion, and the atmosphere resembles a locker room after beating Michigan. If they didn't stay so quiet during the consecration, you might think they came only for the hugging and butting.

It's true that motives for attending Mass are mixed; it is the biggest hall event of the week. There is an area of intersection between dorm brotherhood and religious community where faith is secondary for some. However, in order to hear the Word of God, the first requirement is that a person gets him or herself into a pew, chair, or floor space.

Most of us in Holy Cross are pragmatists about students' motives and are willing to work with those less than pure. After all, that's part of how I got here. I make it a point to note several times per year that there is a future rector sitting out there in the crowd during my turn at post-communion announcements. They don't laugh; a few look scared. The latter I monitor closely and stuff vocation literature in their mailboxes.

In my fourth year in Sorin, fifty out of fifty-seven freshmen attended our opening Mass in August, more than the number of Catholics. I knew that because I had only put out forty-eight of the medals blessed for distribution at the campus-wide Orientation Mass the week before. There were at least twenty more students of all classes in attendance at that Mass compared to the previous year, standing at the back or sitting on the floor of the main aisle. Attendance trails off as some come initially just to see what it's about, but later in the year, it is still not unusual to watch latecomers search in vain for a pew seat.

At that first Orientation Mass celebrated by the University president in the Joyce Center (basketball arena), the first-year men and women are asked to sit on the floor while parents are directed to the stands. The separation deliberately symbolizes the imminent departure of the folks and the start of their children's final march to adult glory. Almost everyone, Catholic and non-Catholic alike, attends that one too.

They mostly show up just two days later for another Mass in the same arena for all classes to celebrate the opening of the academic year, followed with a picnic and fireworks on the quad. We aren't pagans, but we are a bit shameless about using bread and circuses to encourage participation in our spiritual exercises – or sometimes just steaks, cards, and footballs.

*   *   *

I worked with a Campus Ministry Freshman Retreat team last year. A few of its sophomore members had been visiting the Grotto faithfully each week with friends they met on one the year before. One of them told me they usually ran into Brady Quinn, our quarterback for four years, there. I'd heard from a number of sources that he really was a good, well-grounded guy, despite all the hype and glory that surrounds a Heisman trophy nominee. Most Grotto regulars usually are, so I presume it must be true about him.

The Grotto is all rock, iron fence, and candleholders overgrown by some ivy. It was constructed in 1896 with a donation from a diocesan priest from Oil City, Pennsylvania, who was an alumnus. It is one-seventh the size of the Lourdes grotto in France where the Blessed Mother appeared to St. Bernadette. In 1985 after a football game against Michigan, it caught fire.

At 3:00 AM in the waning hours of a Saturday night, calls to the firehouse from students screaming "The Grotto's on fire" were assumed to be the result of pranksters having consumed too much firewater. It took a few more rings for the truck to get rolling, but sure enough, the Grotto was indeed aflame. It seems that the Basilica staff had switched from glass to cheaper plastic candleholders the previous week. There were a record number of pilgrims offering prayers for victory earlier that day, and the mass of candles coagulated into a waxen mound that spontaneously combusted.

The flames started burning off ivy and raced up toward the trees above. The firemen were appropriately reluctant to aim hoses at the Grotto. It was akin to breaking the stained glass windows in a church ablaze, but the only real damage was one large dislodged rock. It was easy enough to clean off the soot and reseal the loose sections, though it was sobering to have a black Madonna for a few days until a cleaning crew could get to it.

There is a book called *Grotto Stories* that has been selling well at the Notre Dame Bookstore for years. My own personal favorite falls under the heading of sublime. About ten years ago, I was walking back from my old office in Moreau Seminary after a post-Christmas blizzard that had dumped twenty-seven inches of snow overnight with six- foot high drifts blocking building entrances. The students were on break, and campus was deserted other than a few of us remaining behind in Corby Hall, emergency personnel, and snow plow drivers.

The temperature was hovering a few degrees below zero, and a light snow was falling in sharp crystals as I walked toward the Grotto. Aside from the days after the fire, it was the first time I had seen the Grotto entirely engulfed in darkness. A howling wind had blown out all the candles, and a chill ran down my back. The Grotto is the heart of the campus, the ember of Christ's light that burns perpetually on campus like the sanctuary lamp next to a church's tabernacle. But that night it looked like a black hole, as I would imagine the dreariness of Hell in the middle of Dante's frozen lake.

I hurried forward at a trot determined to reignite the flame as quickly as possible, and not until I got a few feet in front of the iron fence in front did I see six candles huddled together on the ground. They were tucked behind a boulder shielded from the swirling wind. I'm not quick to think Satan is hiding behind every bush, but it crossed my mind that he might have personally sent a blast our way while our guard was down. I breathed easier and was both relieved and inspired that some faithful soul among the few bodies on campus, probably one of our campus police officers, had seen fit to guard the flame.

It is rare to sit at the Grotto without seeing someone come by to kneel down and light a candle, even at three in the morning on a weeknight. I am always edified by the devotion of our students who keep vigil almost without ceasing. Nevertheless, I also treasure those rare moments when I am all alone there for a few minutes with the Mother of God to celebrate that we are never bereft no matter how dark the night.

The day before classes start in August, the hall staff and I gather all the Sorin freshmen on our front porch at 11:45 PM for their "First Trip to the Grotto." A few think it's too late and go to bed. By the end of the week, they are permanently cured of any hopes of getting to sleep before midnight while they have an address with "Sorin College" in it. We began to do this my first year in the hall. It mirrors the seniors' "Last Trip to the Grotto" on Thursday before Commencement.

Ours is a much simpler affair. I give a short speech about the Grotto, then rehearse the Alma Mater a couple times on the front porch before herding them down. I tell them to walk inside the fence and light a candle. It's a two dollar donation but I tell them their first time is on the house. I care more about encouraging return visits; we get enough money out of them once they become alumni. Then I tell them to say a prayer.

Once they are done we gather off to the side, form a circle, link arms, and sing the Alma Mater quietly, partially to avoid disturbing others there to pray but also because they haven't yet mustered the confidence of the Vienna Boys' Choir. I provide song sheets though after this first time they never need them again. For some, it sets a pattern of devotion which results in regular visits for the next four years.

I am always touched to watch them kneeling with folded hands and bowed heads. It reminds me of First Communion, perhaps because they grow younger each year. I always spot a couple with tears in their eyes and wonder if those are signs of joy at having made it to their dream school or trepidation about the obstacle course ahead.

*   *   *

While there are few prayers more fervent than those of a freshman as midnight tolls to signal his or her first day of class at Notre Dame, one notable exception was on 9/11. The Grotto was packed with a constant flow of traffic all day and all night, like a football weekend but frighteningly somber without the buzz and flashbulbs.

I remember a priest friend studying at a top ten university talking about that day some weeks afterward. He reported that when the news started flashing across campus, people ran out of classroom buildings and dormitories in circles of chaos and confusion. He said they simply did not know where to congregate at first, although he did spot many at the campus ministry center later.

Here, classes were canceled that morning shortly after the hijacked planes crashed into the World Trade Center and Pentagon but before the last plunged into a Pennsylvania field. Then-president Father Malloy convened a meeting of University officers as students began instinctively heading toward the Basilica, the Grotto, or the hall chapels after first getting on their cell phones to check on family and friends.

At 3:00, on five hours notice, a stage was set up next to the flagpole on the South Quad with a sound system, a choir, and vestments for about one hundred concelebrants, one of whom had discovered a few hours earlier that his niece had been a stewardess on United flight 175. We had also received word that a C.S.C. priest had been on the same flight. Thousands filled the quad on a singularly clear and intensely bright September day, but beyond the quad, the rest of the campus was almost as barren as the tundra-like days during Christmas break.

The most profound moment of that Mass for me came at the end after the final hymn, as the concelebrants filed two by two down the makeshift altar steps toward the Knights of Columbus building about one hundred yards away. We had to pass along the edge of the crowd, and no one moved or uttered a sound. Everyone turned to look at us as we passed, like they wanted an answer to the why question no theologian could adequately answer. Not a hair on a head seemed to flutter until we had all entered into the K of C to hang up our vestments. It was chilling, and at that moment I realized a cog had slipped in the cosmos. Only after it was clear that no more words were forthcoming, did they slowly drift away, but crowds streamed back and forth to the Grotto in a constant flow throughout the night.

Many of our Catholic students are woefully ignorant about the catechetical pillars of the faith that I learned in fourth grade. Reality is spending hours on Facebook updating profiles and checking out party postings for the weekend. Some critics think we should do more foundational work in theology classes before lecturing to them about the historical-critical method of Scriptural analysis. They might be right, although I still think limiting their hours of computer access might do almost as much good for their spiritual lives.

The world moves much faster than when I was a child, but most of ours still put down their laptops and slow down for Sunday Mass, including a fair number who are members of other faiths. Hundreds, even star athletes, trek to the Grotto when they feel the darkness pressing in. I also watch a few walking every day down the hallway outside my room, with or without shoes, toward our own chapel to spend a few moments alone with God. Sometimes they shame me with the consistency of their devotion.

No, I don't much care what they wear in church so long as they are continually drawn to it. Etiquette details we can work on gradually over time. The priorities are to dedicate ourselves to the Eucharist, take them on retreats, introduce them to the Grotto, and keep our doors open at odd hours so that they know there is little that can't and won't be forgiven an impulsive nature, especially when they come home safely.

Things change so much so quickly, and their time here is little more than a way station on a long, uncertain journey. Still, it is a place where they can find peace and hope and confidence that they will never be alone or forgotten so long as someone is here to tend the flame and help them to pray. It may be their misfortune to live in an era of online friends who spend more time than they should nurturing superficially constructed self-images.

Still, I think those they live with during their four years in the Dome's shadow and the Grotto's light are the relationships that will endure beyond all technological illusions of intimacy.

Hopefully, they know that we too are here to extend the friendship of Christ to them. Even if at times they test our patience and we fail them at times through our own grievous faults, we have backup. Her patience is inexhaustible.

CHAPTER 11

TRAGEDY AND TRIUMPH

MOST TRADITIONS DON'T ENDURE FOR LONG, even at a place where the word itself is sacred. We do have the nation's first marching band which is now one of the country's largest, but the Marian processions we used to have around campus to implore the intercession of the Blessed Mother against fire ceased more than forty years ago. We've also lost several buildings to fire since we quit formally calling upon her to look out for us. It might be time to resurrect that devotion too.

Whenever we bury a Holy Cross priest or brother, we exit the Basilica and process past the Grotto down St. Mary's Road toward the community cemetery. Until 1990, Holy Cross Hall stood on a small hill along the way. In front is a field that served as its practice ground for interhall football or more informal games of baseball or softball. As the funeral procession passed, the athletes would spontaneously get down on one knee and wait for it to pass.

It's a small thing, but I regret that the Hogs' ritual has joined the list of lost traditions for it symbolized how well Notre Dame students do instinctively gravitate toward the appropriate response likely to be found in an old book on Catholic etiquette. One would have expected it of an earlier generation used to requesting Father's blessing before he left their grammar school classroom, but our students often get it right even without prior training, except of course for their t-shirts. They also rise to the occasion when death hits closer to home.

Almost fifteen years ago, while I was stationed in Portland, a Notre Dame student's mother died without warning from an aneurysm. It was also a time Notre Dame was getting a good deal of negative press for its difficulties navigating landmines – struggling to find the correct balance among the conflicting demands of gridiron success, academic standards, athletic revenues, and student-athlete behavior. The student's older brother, who was not an alumnus, felt compelled to write a letter to the editor of a national publication describing the "real" Notre Dame.

He recounted how his brother's rector responded to the news. He went upstairs and suggested going for a walk. Before heading out, he made a phone call. When the two of them returned to the dorm, awaiting them was an official who expressed his condolences on behalf of the University. He then handed over an envelope containing a plane ticket so the student could fly home immediately. He was grateful but said that he had hoped to travel with another brother living in Chicago. He was handed another envelope with that one's name on it. It held a second ticket for the adjoining seat. No one ever asked for repayment.

However, the older brother who wrote the letter was most

incredulous at the funeral parlor to discover that a significant contingent of his brother's hallmates, along with that same priest, had caravanned for fourteen hours to make it for the wake. That letter demonstrated to me – even before my own later experience of watching friends Tony didn't know he had show up in the chapel for his grandmother's Mass – that we do a reasonable job of teaching students to care for one another when it matters most. It is part of the Holy Cross charism that we pass onto them.

I have been at times overawed by the way we show up in droves for the funerals of fellow community members – and other University members as well. I know that my former neighbors in St. Gabe's parish were floored when fifteen concelebrating priests marched up the aisle at my own dad's funeral. Some of them were not my closest friends, but they drove those eighty-nine and a half miles down the Indiana Toll Road through a horrific early morning thunderstorm to stand with me. Sometimes it is all we can do – and the very best thing to do – to just show up and be there for one another. It is the basis of our lessons about presence that we pass on to RAs that filter down to the rest of our students too.

*   *   *

Nevertheless, there have been two funerals I could not make that I wanted badly to attend. One was the funeral Mass in 1995 for Rev. John Gerber, C.S.C., the seminary rector I tussled with so much, but I was in Portland at the time. He died on Easter Sunday, and the death toll, the deep heavy bell that rings every

163

ten seconds when one of us dies, went out over campus in the midst of the joyous peal of all the bells proclaiming the Easter Alleluia.

The other took place in Corvallis, Oregon, a little more than two years after I had returned to Notre Dame. It was nearing Christmas, and I could not get a flight. For my first two years at the University of Portland, from 1992-94, I was in charge of Christie Hall. It was also that University's first student residence, built in 1911, a little smaller than Sorin but with a nearly identical floor plan.

During my fourth year there, I had changed jobs. I was no longer in charge of the hall but had moved to the second floor as a resident priest. Thad and his roommate JB lived across the hall from me. JB was a committed Catholic with an evangelical bent and Thad was a falling-away one pretending badly to be an agnostic, but that routine became difficult to swallow once he started showing up to weekly Mass in the hall with some regularity. The more frequently I saw him in the pews, the more he liked to prod me with random questions about religion and the Catholic Church specifically. In fact, it would be more appropriate to say that he just liked to harass me generally no matter what the subject.

At one point, early in his second semester as a sophomore, Thad got on a roll, bounding into my room to tell me the latest priest jokes he'd heard, not all of which I found amusing. After about a week, it culminated by him popping into my room four or five times in the same night to tell me yet another. I was getting a little weary of his exuberance and at about 1:15 AM was getting ready for bed. I had closed the door which should have been a hint that I was done listening. Then he came in one more time without knocking, and I yelled out, "What now?"

"You tell me one," he said.

"What?!"

"You tell me a priest joke, and I'll leave."

Now I'm terrible at remembering jokes – maybe about five total that I've heard over the course of my entire life, and three of those are about Cub fans. So, I racked my brain and couldn't think of any except for one I didn't want to tell. I did want him out of my hair.

"OK, you'll really go – for good – if I tell you just one?" I asked.

"Yeah, I'll leave."

"Alright, then. What did the proctologist say to the priest after his operation?" "I dunno. What?" he asked.

"'The ass is mended. Go in peace.' Now get out of my room."

He walked out smiling and I turned back to grab my sweater off my recliner on the way to my bedroom. Then the door opened. Again no polite knock, he just bounded in, and there was Thad standing in my kitchen yelling, "I want to hear you tell it again." Sophomores! I grabbed all sixty-five inches of him by his shirt collar, opened the door, tossed him out into the hallway, and deadbolted the door behind me. He pounded on it for about five minutes, but I ignored him and went to bed.

The next year I was assigned to direct Portland's foreign study program in Salzburg and was thereby relieved from joke duty along with theological questions that inevitably required long answers, at least from him if not my overseas crowd. I was, however, pleased to hear the following March that Thad had decided to stay on campus and had been accepted as an RA in the fall.

I returned from Austria a couple of months later and prepared to move back to Notre Dame. I had been appointed our community's vocation director and only spent a couple of weeks back in Portland before packing up. After I put nine boxes, a set of golf clubs, a wooden rocking chair that I'd refinished, a couple of suitcases and gym bags into a U-Haul, Thad was there to see me off. He was the last person I saw waving as I circled around to head out to Interstate 84.

A couple weeks before the next semester was scheduled to start in August, I got a call from JB. Thad was not going to be an RA or returning to school. He had been having severe headaches that summer, and doctors discovered a tumor behind his eyeball pinching the optic nerve. They were going to start with chemotherapy in hopes of shrinking the tumor for surgery enough to save his left eye. However, after several weeks of treatment, the doctors decided to operate and removed it.

I flew out to Portland and drove down to his home in Corvallis the first week in November with JB to see him. He was weak from the chemo, surgery, and a round of radiation they had started after discovering signs that the tumor had spread to a couple of lymph nodes. He and his family were confident that he would go into remission after the treatments.

Thad was lying in bed when I walked into his house, and his girlfriend was sitting next to him. He was mostly bald and in place of his left eye, he had a six inch long scar. He hadn't lost his sense of humor and tried to crack jokes but was quite weak and was only able to sit up briefly. His family was hopeful, but I was fairly certain it would be the last time I saw him. I regretted that I could not acknowledge it in the face of everyone else's optimism.

About six weeks later, I got another call from JB. Thad had been experiencing some pain in his legs and had gone in for an MRI. The cancer had metastasized throughout his body, and it moved with vengeance. A few days later he died, and JB phoned once again to break the news but not quite as I expected. The pastor of his parish was also the auxiliary bishop of Portland and had gone to administer the Sacrament of the Sick to Thad the previous day. He was in considerable pain and unable to converse much, but near the end of the visit he turned to JB and said, "I want to hear him say it."

"What?"

"The punch line."

"What punch line?"

"You know, the priest joke."

With some reluctance, JB went up to the bishop seated at Thad's bedside, gulped before his pectoral cross, and said, "Tell Thad, 'The ass is mended, go in peace.'"

"Um, what?" asked the bishop, not a little perplexed.

"Just say it." said JB.

So the bishop shrugged, and since he was a kindly man, not in the habit of refusing deathbed requests that were harmless if a little odd, leaned over to Thad, and said into his ear, "Thad, the ass is mended, go in peace."

Thad looked over at JB and said, "See, I got a bishop to say it." He smiled, then closed his eyes, lapsed into a coma, and died later that day in the company of JB and his parents. Those were the last words he spoke. As the bishop was leaving, JB tried to explain to the context of the joke to him, but I imagine he left wondering what was going on with the priests at the University of Portland.

After JB finished this account, I was dumbstruck for a moment and then began to laugh, and so did he who had just lost his best friend. There are more inspiring stories about saints who have discovered grace through suffering. Still, it is awfully hard to think of many other ways that two people could find themselves convulsed in laughter before shedding tears together over a twenty one year old's death from cancer just hours earlier. Thad had dropped out confirmation class during high school because of friction between him and the instructor and nearly drifted away from the Church, but at the end, he had the sole attention of a bishop who confirmed his faith and prepared him for the life to come.

I know I didn't get ordained to tell punch lines attributed to proctologists to be repeated at someone's deathbed by a prelate. However, I firmly believe that God must have a quirky sense of humor too and that when people go to heaven they don't lose their personalities but become even fuller creations of who they were on earth. I am confident and at peace in the knowledge Thad is bursting regularly and gleefully through the doors of the Heavenly Palace, impudently telling God jokes to the Almighty – and getting picked up by the scruff of his neck and tossed down the golden stairs at least every seventh day when even He needs some rest. Whenever I think of Thad, I laugh for a long time, just like on that December night when the call I was expecting came, before the tears begin to form. I would say to him, "rest in peace," but I have no hope that heaven has been peaceful ever since that pesky little guy got through the gates.

It is a strange life we live, noting the insolent ways of undergraduates one day, trying to connect with them as they bow their heads earnestly in the chapel the next, and often hugging some shifting ground in between. I know it is a confusing time for them as they waffle in uncertainty attempting to forge identities and personalities. It is not that they are entirely different than the rest of us, just that the paradoxes are more obvious, the tragedies and triumphs grounded in starker relief.

CHAPTER 12

THE VIEW FROM THE PORCH

BEHIND THE SWINGS OF SORIN'S FRONT PORCH are names randomly scratched into the bricks. They are predominantly last names and nicknames along with class years of our graduates. Some go back many years and are barely legible while the markings of others are quite fresh. They just appear out of nowhere when people like me aren't looking, though I actually have no complaint about graduates leaving their final mark during Senior Week. It is, I think, a grand hall tradition – for the most part.

However, one May day I discovered that one of the quietest and meekest RAs I've known not only carved his name in the middle of the night but filled it in with black marker. From a hundred yards away, it was more visible than our two porch swings, so the next day I sat there conducting a stake out. When he approached with a couple of accessories, I pulled a large screwdriver out of my back pocket and with raised eyebrows said, "It looks like you tagged the front porch" before handing him the tool. He looked down at his feet and said, "Yeah, I guess it was a bit much." Then I sat there swinging leisurely on

171

the porch, enjoying the spring warmth with a book as he spent some of his last precious moments at Notre Dame carving out every granule that had been saturated with black marker.

Actually, I did him a favor. The additional digging will guarantee that his name will last for at least several additional decades. Nearly ten years ago, the University cleaned the bricks of both Sorin and Corby Hall, and the pencil scratchings of students hoping to leave their mark that had survived for nearly a century were washed away. I've always regretted we weren't a little more understanding that the grime and gritty imperfections we've accumulated on our walls are part of our legacy too.

As far as I'm concerned, the graduating Otters can carve away and be remembered so long as Notre Dame bricks remain stacked together on old prairie land, but don't dare use ink! The squirrels are, for whatever reason, actually eating entire bricks at ground level. I figure they're doing a lot more damage than to the building than scratching Otters.

It isn't unusual for RAs to go a bit wayward, releasing their pent-up desires for a little rebellion, in their final days. That's why, unlike the rest of the year, I keep my door closed during Senior Week trying mighty hard not to hear what I don't want to know about what's going on upstairs. By that time, they're mentally out of here. Forget fines, shame, lectures, eyebrow raising, or humor. There are nine days between the end of finals week and Commencement, and seniors don't have many exams. Some wind up with two or three weeks at the end of the semester with little to do except contemplate the sad reality that their time is nearly up.

Theoretically, they should be thrilled. They are about to receive a first class diploma and gain access to the world's most loyal alumni network. Friendships have been formed that will last a lifetime. Most will be wed with former hallmates standing beside them as groomsmen and bridesmaids. In fact, spouses have been known to comment about how they married not only their partner but his or her hall. Nevertheless, Senior Week is the most depressing one of the year.

I have grown accustomed to hearing tough Otters sniffle and watching them pretend to rub dirt specks out of their eyes at their last hall Mass in May. I've also warned them on occasion that their feelings will be quite mixed as the days of Senior Week progress. At the very moment the Commencement ceremony ends and their Notre Dame careers reach their apotheosis, they are hit with the reality that they will never all be together again. The ones accepted to grad schools and firms are lucky, but the unemployed and drifting can leave fearing they have been cast cruelly into the creek of life heading upstream.

Parents arrive for that weekend wanting to celebrate one more set of paid tuition bills being tossed into the fire, but their children are less pleased to stand for hours in cap and gown for photos. They endure nicely organized, classy dinners, waiting anxiously for their folks to wear out so they can sneak off to the nearby Linebacker Lounge for a few final belts with their friends scattering across the continents.

Occasionally, they wallow in denial and despite having days to pack, do not begin until after graduating. I have known of angry parents screaming at their sons because they need to be at work the next morning and planned on getting home to Pittsburgh by midnight while the newly-minted graduate hasn't even begun to empty his dresser drawers. They show up in overloaded cars one August fearful of letting go of a child, then drive off four years later ticked off at the grown one they are carting back.

There are notable and touching examples of the opposite extreme. Another rector told me of a student who gave his diploma to his parents in gratitude for everything they had sacrificed for him. I make that suggestion now too. I tell seniors, "Think about it. After all, your parents paid for it."

As an alternative, I suggest they make an appointment to see Father Hesburgh, bring along a copy of his autobiography, *God, Country, and Notre Dame,* ask him to autograph it, then hand that to the folks on Commencement Day. A few have. Every other blue moon, someone heeds my advice. Most parents and graduates do leave happy and mutually grateful. It's just awful though when the culmination of four years is an ugly public scene.

*   *   *

The view from the porch changes with the seasons but the pattern varies little over the years. For ten days after Commencement and before summer school begins, there is barely a student to be seen. It should be a placid time for reading Joyce, Plato, or Aquinas, contemplating deep thoughts without fear of interruption, but it is not. As soon as vans and SUV's depart laden with new graduates, along with more Notre Dame clothing and illegally garnered souvenirs than when they first arrived, tour buses start heading to the heart of Indiana's top tourist destination.

They park at the Bookstore. The school kids, senior citizens, and other assorted vacationers eventually are drawn to the Dome, Basilica, and Grotto all just beyond Sorin. They stop frequently to ask questions: "Can you tell me how I get back to the Bookstore?" "Where is the Grotto from here?" "Is that Knute Rockne on top of the Dome?" I trust that the Blessed Mother looking down on them from the top has a sense of humor. It is easy to tell the lifelong subway alums who know more facts from the Notre Dame encyclopedia than I do from the merely curious one-shot tourists.

The Sorin porch is a brilliant spot for watching the flowers bloom in summer, cheering the football team in fall as they emerge from Mass on Saturday mornings on their way to the stadium, or doing crosswords while keeping an eye on freshmen. At no time of the year is it a place to concentrate on serious work. All roads lead to Sorin. One can hardly ignore it on the way to the Basilica, which has become more of a pilgrimage destination since it received that official designation from Pope John Paul II in 1992. People regularly pause right in front of our porch during all seasons to have their picture taken with its spire in the background. On football weekends, you can stand out there and easily determine whether the opponents have a large proportion of Catholic fans by watching how many pass through the Basilica's portals with their orange, green, or red jackets.

In September 2000, Notre Dame loyalists were amazed to walk into the Stadium and find half the fans wearing Nebraska red. There was outrage in the student newspaper afterward about the unfaithful alumni who scalped tickets, but there is another side of the story.

A few months before I'd received a phone call from the Sister of Mercy who was my grade school principal in Chicago. She inquired sweetly – actually rather commandingly – about whether I could possibly dig up four football tickets for relatives coming to the game. Well, I had four, and how does one say no to an eighty-three-year- old nun who has intimidated you all your life? I didn't make a profit on the tickets, and I suspect many other alums got innocently bushwhacked too.

But I heard many remarks afterwards like, "Those Nebraska people were the nicest fans we ever had here." The Cornhuskers may be diehards about football, but an awful large contingent toured the Basilica too. There is a strong correlation between how friendly visiting folk are and their dual interest in making the trek as pilgrims and fans.

However, those football weekends also bring a crowd that ventures up Sorin's front steps only because they are desperately looking for a bathroom. Because it is not unusual for our residents to step out into the hallway in the morning and find a line of strangers wearing green and gold knit beanies outside the first-floor john, I have taken to putting up gently worded signs on the porch pillars, "Public restrooms are located directly behind the Basilica" with an arrow pointing north. It doesn't deter many. While the front door is locked, there is a constant traffic flow in and out, so anyone who waits ten seconds gets in.

I have to admit that the signs may also be a little incongruous on the hospitality scale with the "Sorin Mass ½ hour after the game" posters directly above. I don't appreciate picking up the beer bottles left behind on the steps and in the grass of my front yard either, though I am grateful for the $5,000-6,000 total collection money the more polite Mass attendees do part with after seven games for the benefit of St. Jude School in Uganda. It makes no difference to me whether they cheer for Notre Dame or our opponents.

A week and a half after Commencement, graduate students working on a teaching degree through the Alliance for Catholic Education (ACE) start arriving on campus. Some come from other colleges, but many just left here as degreed Domers. They inevitably return disconcerted. I told one RA about to start the program after he'd received his diploma, "You'll be gone barely a week and a half, but it will seem like you've been away for a year and a half when you get back."

He didn't know what I meant, but after he returned, he agreed that while he had come back to a place that should have been familiar, he felt more like he was starting over as a freshman. He knew a few in his cohort; however, his closest friends were gone, and he was staying in another dorm that wasn't home. It is tough to feel like a stranger because the place changes immediately after graduation even if the names engraved in brick do remain.

*   *   *

Originally, Sorin College did not have a front porch. The architects' drawings actually show two rather impressive Victorian porches, one on the east front and the other on the north, but the wings were truncated during construction in 1888 and both scrapped. Money was likely the issue; it usually was when the University operated out of a cigar box that was filled with more IOUs than legal tender. Even nine years later, when simpler north and south wings were added, no porch was affixed to the building's east façade.

Then the following decade, in 1905, Colonel William Hoynes, who was probably nothing more than a water boy in the Civil War but looked the part, was strolling out the front door one day from the law school he had founded in Sorin the same year the extra rooms were added to the rear. He was on his way to the Washington Hall theater for a gala event decked out in topcoat and tails. The Colonel didn't get there, at least in that outfit, as some overly exuberant youths tossed a bucket of ice water upon him from what is now a freshman quad on the third floor.

The roof constructed over the porch soon afterward to prevent repeat performances bequeathed to us the best vantage point on campus to rock in the shade and watch God Quad tulips bloom – and witness frisky Otters whack off their buds with wayward Frisbee tosses. I repose there often, blissfully content that no freshman a century later could fall prey to a fleeting temptation to douse his rector with ice, although I have been embraced by a horde intent on a group hug after sliding around in the mud out back. I am also invariably pleased whenever I have the opportunity to greet an old Otter on a visit to his former home climbing our steps, pointing out to his son, daughter, or grandchild his name etched proudly into our bricks.

CHAPTER 13

Home Cooking

THE CLASSIC JOKE IS: Dad comes to visit and marvels about the expansion of choices in the dining hall. He turns to his son and says, "This is great. You have twelve different options to choose from for dinner."

"Yeah," says the son, "but they're the same twelve every day."

A generation and a half ago, we filed into the end of one of three lines and had a choice between mystery meat with instant mashed potatoes and a crusty casserole. I never once opted for the dreadful dish known as Hungarian Noodle Bake. Dessert was dry white cake or a pudding that looked like plastic goop out of a factory vat. The scuttlebutt was that the food service operation that had the contract here provided four different levels of service with four being the best – and we had minus one.

In fact, by mixing and matching, there are more than twelve offerings in each food group, from Jello to jambalaya. Many of them are the same each day, but I do see different protein offerings whenever I go in there. I can even look at the meat being custom carved on the cutting board by a chef and rest assured that it didn't arrive on the loading dock with jockey marks on its rump. Overall, they complain less than we did, but even when they do, I'm convinced that the food isn't the problem so much as the mess hall ambience. Three or four hundred people nudging one another with trays like longhorns in the pasture all trying to get to the big muddy at the same time just doesn't feel like sitting down for Mom's home cooking.

They really can't be that picky about what they shovel in. Some order pizza three or four nights a week and pump it in like gas into a Hummer. There is a Papa John's outlet a few blocks away that serves only Notre Dame and St. Mary's students. It just goes to show there are easy ways to make money even if my business professor friends claim otherwise. If it's true that there are three main preoccupations for college-age males, i.e., sex, booze, and food, we have to make the most of the only need to which we can legitimately cater. For quite some time, rectors have been using vittles to bribe them into stopping by to check in with us.

Father George used to take his staff and hall government out for a very nice Christmas dinner, preceded by a tasteful soiree in his room featuring eggnog laced with fine brandy and cognac. He's the only guy I ever saw waste Courvoisier on sophomores. Then the '80s ended, and he got called on the carpet for being an illegal provider. Personally, I think we'd be in a lot better shape if we could train our charges to sit in our rooms and sip $8 a cup Christmas nog with us whatever the law says. I know – I'm just dreaming.

During my third year in Sorin, I was casting about for some way to boost daily Mass attendance. We were averaging about three per night. I have an electric range the size of a postage stamp and virtually no counter space, so I had to cook something that could be thrown in one big pot. With a few exceptions, beans are a favorite, and they like them hot. Voila! The Sorin College Chili Mass was born.

The first time I made the recipe half a bowl made me sweat, and my nose ran. I considered packaging it as a decongestant. It was quite amusing to watch a few Otters put in ten more splashes of Tabasco anyway. Like I said earlier, they're human garbage disposals. That first year we averaged about fifteen per Mass, and the following year more like thirty. The only problem is that now I'm locked into cooking five gallons of chili every two weeks except on Ash Wednesday. The individual record is ten bowls. I sometimes wonder if I'm just enabling gluttony, but it works.

In a more perfect world, I'd prefer more natural piety, but it's no different from thousands of parish youth groups that are using paintball and toboggan outings to get high school kids into church. I would be more concerned if attendance had declined since the first year of Chili Mass, but it has been creeping up on Sundays, too. I like to think at least a few are being fed in church, too.

*   *   *

And then, there's Miss Leitha who cooks an even bigger pot of chili for those she calls her "babies" in O'Neill Family Hall during finals week. She once put on a complete soul food meal for the entire hall of 271 residents, and I was hard put to make the collard greens I was tasked with serving last to the end of the line. The current rector, Ed Mack, added the "Miss" after he arrived in 2002, my last of four years in that hall, because he quickly recognized who was really in charge over there. Miss Leitha calls everyone her "Baby," including Ed and her resident priests.

It's such a habit, she slipped one day during a summer retreat and addressed our local bishop in the same manner as he wandered by. She did come up with a quick "Oops," but I think he was wise enough to consider it a compliment, as well he should. She rules O'Neill with an iron broom and a sassy sweet attitude that encourages instant compliance. No one messes with Miss Leitha. She feeds those guys *every* day – by getting them to behave better than they would otherwise and making them like it. They know she cares about her babies, and just to be there and to be cared for is what they value most. When she retires in a few months, the O'Neill guys may get another efficient broom, but the attitude is irreplaceable.

My next door neighbor, Monk, gets into the act too. His cooking skills end somewhere just past making tea, and he doesn't even have a hot plate in his room. In fact, he doesn't have a real mattress either but sleeps on a daybed. He takes all the freshmen in Sorin out to dinner in groups of five before fall break in October. Of course, a president emeritus has a lot bigger budget than I do.

Monk will leave that room lying on a stretcher holding tightly to a book when he's about eighty-nine. I don't think I'll last that long. I know it would have driven me crazy to live in a one-room residence hall condo while serving as president for eighteen years. His is a monkish existence, surrounded by walls thirteen feet high filled with books. That example of faithful and humble service is a way of feeding our young Otter pups too, even if it takes years for some to appreciate the sacrifice made by someone who could easily lead a more leisurely life. Whenever Monk is in, he gladly posts a hand-written envelope on his door with the word "Welcome." Later they will realize how much little things like that make a dorm feel more like a home.

*   *   *

Finals week has gotten better since we've gone to four study days before the first one. Rectors don't like it because many spend the first two days going to off-campus parties and bars, which is not the use academic officers who approved the change envisioned. Nevertheless, the stress level seems much reduced from previous years. Part of the reason is grade inflation. The other is that even if they don't use the time efficiently, they aren't under a gun with a four-day cushion, so they don't freak out from the pressure. You see a lot of Mountain Dew being consumed during finals week by procrastinators, but I don't see so many these days mainlining No-Doze.

I do my part. I start off healthy, serving chicken soup before the first night of finals. Then I give myself a break from sweating over the stove and go to the other extreme by making a run for seven dozen Krispy Kremes the next day. Meatball subs or black bean soup follows with chili once again on Wednesdays. I know what it's like to work at a school cafeteria when there is a line outside my door ten minutes before the chow is served. And forget about leftovers.

*   *   *

A Notre Dame student today should look at the future like a menu in a Chinese restaurant: lots of options, most pretty good, hard to choose just one, better to share. It was one thing for our grandparents to take any job they could get in a factory to feed the pack of kids at home. They were lucky if they had a few dimes to rub together after loading up on oatmeal and spaghetti, at least if I can trust my mother who swears she survived on that diet for weeks at a time. The word "options" wasn't part of their vocabulary.

It's another to spend years chained to a desk expecting the kids you don't know to be grateful for their Ivy League-quality educations and summer vacations in Europe. Harry Chapin had a hit with "Cat's in the Cradle" that everyone my age can sing along with, but I'm afraid the lessons found within those lyrics will never sink entirely into any generation's consciousness. It irks me whenever someone walks into my room and says, "I want to go to law school so I can make enough money to raise a family and send my kids to Notre Dame." Great, if they want to be lawyers – or biologists, doctors, engineers, or musicians. Sometimes they come in hoping for the response I give: "Do what you love rather than working at something the rest of your life that makes your family miserable because you hate it and

184

impose your resentments upon them when you come home at night." It's a canned line. I've used it often.

I'd rather have them temporarily paralyzed by the multitude of menu choices because they are privileged enough to be acquiring an education that enables them to have so many once they leave rather than feeling locked into a predestined fate. It doesn't matter whether the pressure is generated internally or externally from stage-mother parents who think a college degree is merely the means to a huge stock portfolio or simply won't hear of them forsaking the family business.

I will admit that I'm not paying their tuition; I've never cleaned a diaper; many of them are bigger than me; and I know – they're not really kids anymore. I don't have to pay fourteen percent more every year for health insurance, or get called upon to answer an eight year old when he asks "Why don't we have a Lexus too?" But I have seen meltdowns by the ones who cracked under the strain of striving to be something they weren't cut out for and drifted away into non-degree oblivion.

They aced the SAT practice tests since middle school and got all the way here. Then it hits them that they spent the first twenty years of their lives living up to others' expectations rather than looking into their hearts and chasing the dreams within. I do know the ones who leave here happiest are those fortunate to have folks who made time for them and granted them the freedom to become whatever they want. By that time, the kids have also learned a few things about priorities and could care less about what kind of car sits in the garage at home.

Good parenting is a constant balancing act. It doesn't have

to be a zero-sum game, but it is important to have a clear sense about what to do when you can't keep fifteen balls in the air. I am amazed to know a fair number of people who successfully juggle rewarding careers, deposit enough in the college fund to generate tuition money for four or five children, pile up hundreds of thousands of frequent flier miles showing their young ones the world, drive one or more $50,000 cars, and end up with polite, generous, well-adjusted kids. I'm not sure how they do it. I'll admit I couldn't, and I greatly admire those who manage it.

I do sympathize with the families where one parent is working in a factory or with those who are all alone to bear the load. They have good reason to feel stretched. I have less for the Lexus owners who won't allow their kids to pursue their passion for playing the trumpet because music is not a "practical" career. Sometimes when I've finished a conversation with a kid who's feeling pressure from home to become a corporate CEO by the time he hits thirty, I want to give his parents a few words of advice from a priest who doesn't know what he's talking about like:

> *Feed them with love, commitment, faith, generosity, and humility. Teach them that they are among the most fortunate people on the earth and have an obligation to spend their lives giving more back. Take them to Disneyland, but bring them to a soup kitchen or nursing home once in a while too so they take nothing for granted.*

> *Fund their high school excursions to Italy, but make them work summers to pay for their gas money and video games so they understand that they have to earn what they get. Have them do practice tests because there are just some hoops even a seventeen year old must jump*

through, but tell them to revel in reading great literature and take college courses that make their souls sing and open up new worlds they hadn't imagined.

Do spoil them — some. It's impossible not to be a soft touch once in a while if you love someone, but be a parent, not their best buds. They actually respect people who say no to them once in a while even if they don't like it right away.

Embrace your daughter if she comes home pregnant and love her even more, but challenge your sons and daughters to consider what they would like to tell their own children someday about their own sexual activities during college. You don't even have to be religious to understand that we lead by example in all things but most of all in child-rearing.

We gradually lose control as they age and have to let go in order for them to grow, but we can keep asking questions that raise the bar and cause them to ponder more deeply their own choices. Often a student who has a well-developed moral framework, even if it's not the one of my denomination, has all they need to make the right choice and avoid a disaster in a dicey situation.

Some of you will do just about everything right and still get a phone call because your son or daughter got something wrong. Bad things happen to good kids, even in our protective Catholic Eden. The awful, random tragedies are the ones no priest wants to stand in a pulpit trying to explain.

But, most of the time, the apple doesn't fall that far. I don't know whether it's more nature or nurture, but both ways the fruit ripens

187

mainly at home. Since most of them seem to come out pretty well at the end of Senior Week, I figure most of you are good jugglers, but there are the occasional ones who would rather scream into the phone at me than peer deeper inside their own walls to figure out why their kid's life is so fouled up.

Occasionally, I've preached to couples getting married that unless it really is impossible, spend at least one meal a day with everyone at table, even if it has to be a bowl of oatmeal and a couple of donuts in the morning. It was one of our priests, Father Pat Peyton, C.S.C., who coined the phrase, "The family that prays together stays together." Not to put down prayer, but he didn't nail it all; he should have said "prays and eats" together.

I love dining in Italy because meals are sacred times not to be rushed – even among those who no longer pray. The best place to work out the gritty problems in a home is at the family table. When they come for chili on Wednesday nights, they usually chow down and dash out, but every once in a while someone stays to chat who otherwise might have run off to Burger King across the quad for extra protein instead. That's why we use food. It works. It brings them to places where they can be fed in other ways too.

It can be confusing to have so many life paths as options, but that's better than having none at all. Being human means having to make choices and learning to be satisfied without devouring everything on the menu. It isn't easy, but the more we are free to learn, think, study, reflect, soar – and pray – the less likely we are to opt for something we didn't really want.

CHAPTER 14

MARS AND VENUS

WHEN I ARRIVED AT NOTRE DAME IN 1977, the ratio of men to women in my class was about 3:1. Throwing in the totals from St. Mary's College across the road reduced the ratio to approximately 3:2 against. I spent a lot of time at St. Mary's, more than in the women's halls at Notre Dame combined.

I even joined a choir over there to improve my odds. Within my circle of friends, there are almost as many who found spouses on the other side of the road than in the more immediate shadow of the Dome. I still have buried in a box somewhere a picture of a bunch of St. Mary's friends standing behind the antique bar my roommates and I spent a week refurbishing at the start of my junior year. I don't show it around though. We've outlawed bars – another policy change that shows we have grown a little smarter over the years.

Now that the ratio is almost 50-50 at Notre Dame, the dynamics have changed radically. I would go to St. Mary's at least once a week even when I wasn't singing with a group of friends, sometimes just to eat in their dining hall instead of ours. Most

Notre Dame males rarely venture over there now. The numbers of St. Mary's women have declined since the 1970s, though a new president, who is an alumna, has boosted enrollment and is infusing a renewed sense of commitment into the College's mission.

What surprises me is that student complaints about the dating scene don't differ much than when I was an undergraduate. Back then we attributed it to male desperation that there just weren't enough women. Now the men have the numbers advantage with St. Mary's added to the mix, but still "dating" is relatively infrequent.

Every year there is a brief spurt of articles and letters in the campus newspaper questioning whether single-sex dorms and parietal (limits on opposite sex visitation) hours foment awkwardness and retard social development. However, Notre Dame graduates appear to do quite well finding mates once they graduate. If long-term development is the goal, then short-term frustrations result more from the impatience of those of an age who simply don't like being told that they can't do what they want when they want to.

The male-to-female ratio at Notre Dame neared equality at about the same time that college students began to grow more reluctant about dating and gun-shy about commitments in general. The average age for a first marriage in the U.S. is now into the early thirties. I've celebrated some weddings of alumni who dated throughout a good chunk of college and got married within a couple of years after, but generally, people just aren't as anxious about getting a "ring by spring" of their senior year.

It is a pity the guy trying not to be naked five years ago ran into a cop instead of Sister Jean Lenz, O.S.F., the unofficial "First Lady" of Notre Dame. She had her own book, *Loyal Sons and Daughters,* published in 2003. I have been aware as I've been writing that there is no substitute for living with people in getting to know them well, and I have only lived in all-male halls with one exception that I cover in the next chapter. I know this book is definitely skewed toward life on Mars. While Sister Jean's book is broader in scope beyond residential life, if you want the view from Venus, I think she does a pretty good job of compensating for my omissions.

The one tale about Sister Jean that is known by people through years of oral tradition, even more than from her book sales, describes the night that she single-handedly stopped a screaming horde of male streakers from busting through the front doors of Farley Hall. Undergraduate women had just been admitted to Notre Dame in 1972, and she was the hall's first female rector.

She heard a growing rumble that sounded like a gathering of Viking warriors out front on the North Quad and saw her women rush to their windows for a better view. She was a bit discombobulated since naked men hadn't been a regular fixture of convent life; nevertheless, she bravely stepped out on the front porch and shouted out to the leader of the pack: "You are not coming in here like that!" I've yet to meet a guy yet who will run naked past a nun scolding him like a third grader, so naturally they all sneaked away.

A couple of years after her book came out, she mentioned to me that same guy, visiting on a football weekend, had approached her and said, "Remember me?" Of course, she didn't. He seemed disappointed that while his moment in all his glory had made her book, she didn't recognize him in some of his flesh. However, more than thirty years had passed, and he was indeed dressed quite differently.

Father Hesburgh is fond of saying that letting women into Notre Dame was the best decision he ever made because it "humanized" the place. He was right to foresee that daughters could be just as loyal, but the culture on campuses has also changed significantly since then. Perhaps the best one-page article I've ever read appeared in 2006 in the aftermath of the Duke lacrosse scandal. It's called *"Role Reversals: Hazards of the College Party Culture"* by Barbara DaFoe Whitehead. She notes an interesting phenomenon. In contrast to college life a couple of generations ago, gender roles in the social realm have been almost wholly reversed.

Women now predominate on most college campuses while men control the party scene that has substituted an MTV spring break culture for cotillions and formal dances. Whereas couples previously might have snuck away for a few beers and gotten carried away from there, the current dynamic promotes massive consumption of alcohol in large groups and drinking games that reward puking, with clothes shed readily in front of hundreds by both sexes indiscriminately.

College women have been sucked into a social dynamic in which their behavior is increasingly indistinguishable from the frat boys they often outperform in the classroom and later at the office. It is as Whitehead notes, "at odds with their own sense of dignity and self-worth." Instead of humanizing men, they are being increasingly de-humanized by them.

One-page articles don't allow for many nuances, and there may be points to quibble about. Outside of formal dances, males have dominated other social venues for years, the unofficial "old-boy" network of club memberships and golf outings serving as a prime example of how professional and social hierarchies can persist. The author's observations may be a sign that unofficial social barriers providing cover for male misbehavior are much harder to attack than blatantly illegal discrimination and, ultimately, even more controlling.

To my knowledge, there has never been date rape case on the Notre Dame campus that did not involve alcohol as the precipitating factor. On average, a woman of equal body weight to a man will get drunk twice as fast. It is not an arena in which women can hope to compete on an equal footing, yet today's college culture pushes them to compete lustily, swig for swig at the beer pong table. We can limit it on campus, but our reach is limited at a party house a mile away, and we haven't quite figured out how to patrol that scene as closely as we do our own hallways.

*   *   *

When a cholera epidemic was consuming Notre Dame in the mid-1850s, Father Sorin took to burying professors, staff, and Holy Cross religious who fell victim undercover at midnight by candlelight. If word had spread that the mostly forested acreage was a den of pestilence, the school by the lake would have gone under quickly. He didn't have a degree in microbiology but was convinced that a dam across the road on land owned by a crusty protagonist who refused to sell was causing the disease, so Father Sorin marched over to tear it down while the farmer was away.

The image was captured in a rather hackneyed 1960 television pilot for a series called "The Trial," starring Jeffrey Hunter as Sorin. He is depicted standing on a hill, mimicking Charlton Heston's Moses on the brink of the Red Sea and ordering, "Brothers, to the dam!" Sound effect thunder booms and phony lightning bolts flash as obedient religious with pick axes dramatically make the waters flow. Soon thereafter, the landowner decided it would be prudent to make a deal. Father Sorin was proven right, and he got title to a good chunk of what would later become St. Mary's College. The epidemic came to an abrupt end, like the rest of the series itself which was never picked up by a network.

There is little doubt that the entire enterprise would have been wiped out before the Civil War, like Jamestown a couple of centuries earlier, had Father Sorin felt compelled to seek counsel's approval before sending Seabees in cassocks across the road. The thought is tempting, but imagine the lawsuits if we walked down the street in our collars to bust down doors beyond our jurisdiction to rescue vulnerable women doing keg stands at off campus houses?

The law of unintended consequences has struck with a vengeance. Just because a woman can do anything a man can doesn't mean she should try. The self-confident ones don't, but it requires more courage to be a woman in this generation and perhaps in every one. It is a cruel paradox for many who get caught up in today's sex and booze culture, but it is an even greater injustice being perpetrated on the women who inhabit our campuses today.

Maybe I'm just a sexist with a "boys will be boys" mentality, but there are differences between women and men when it comes to alcohol, and a few other things too. I don't think it would be so funny if I had to confront naked coeds in front of my hall and tell them they aren't coming into Sorin College dressed like that, and I don't like seeing panties worn as outerwear. I would be quite surprised if their mothers didn't agree.

I was talking to a female staff member not long ago who told me she understands why so many guys have soft-core porn on their walls when girls walk around campus with wearing fishnet clothing that reveals almost as much as the poster models. Scanty clothing eggs on men's hormonal fantasies and gives them permission to act out in ways that both parties might regret later. I said that if I made that comment as a man, I'd be pilloried. She just nodded her head quietly. It is a devil's dilemma because in both the old days and in the new, for all their achievements in and out of the classroom, women are getting the short end of the stick. I'm just not sure how to apportion the blame.

*   *   *

On the other hand, we have had a couple of women student body presidents, including our first-ever female president and vice-president team in 2007, and even more valedictorians. I also believe that the women in residence halls are more dedicated to doing the grunt work that builds a strong sense of community within them. I know that most of the time whenever a Sorin Otter heads out to the supermarket to pick up supplies for a hall barbeque, I feel compelled to remind him to get what I consider to be essentials – like charcoal – and consider it a victory if he merely forgets lighter fluid or paper plates. In addition to their humanizing qualities, on a practical level, women tend to be better at getting things done.

I'm not a sociologist, but women are better team players too. I notice it on the basketball court. Too many men are hot dogs and live for the slam dunk. The women are more disciplined and play a purer game. Their mechanics are better, and they make fewer mistakes. It's the difference between listening to a symphony and watching a heavy metal band break electric guitar strings. Both can be entertaining but sometimes a person, particularly as he grows older, prefers understatement to mania. I can only conclude that women like rules more than men who rejoice in breaking them.

I sometimes wonder whether the men's dorms would be better off with women rectors and vice versa. As much as I butt heads with male undergrads, a similar dynamic seems to affect most women's halls. One female rector told me that it has something to do with college women's changing relationships with their mothers – they view a rector as a mother substitute at the very stage they are in revolt against their own.

But the same is essentially true for men. Sister Jean's theory is that undergraduate males who have authority issues with their rectors don't get along with their fathers. Looking back at individual cases over the years, I'd have to say that that one holds up pretty well. I wonder whether men and women humanize one another better when social boundaries and authority roles are clearer than anything today's generation has known? Parietals and single-sex residence halls are about the only thing we have left to keep them even momentarily apart.

The funny thing is that numerous men and women tell us that some of their favorite moments at Notre Dame take place after the witching bell of parietals has rung, at midnight or 2:00 AM. on weekends, and they get to sit around relaxing with friends of their own gender, relieved of dating and mating pressures. I'm not always edified by the content of what I hear, but as long as they aren't bellowing profanities that can be heard two floors away, I try to give them their space.

This chapter has been the toughest to write because I know this book is not so much about undergraduate residences at Notre Dame as it is about daily life in the men's halls. I do know that if I were the rector of a women's hall, I would alter my style and suppress some of my inherent crustiness and natural competitiveness. I can be a warm fuzzy when I put my mind to it, even if it's not my default position.

Most men like to be pushed and show what they think of one another indirectly by kidding, pranks, and head-butting one another figuratively and literally. Women generally want people like us to listen intently. They want to feel secure, and they need more attention. While I've had a few men who were seriously depressed or had other psychological issues, as far as I know, I haven't had a bulimic, a cutter, or a suicide attempt in nearly five years here. I've been very fortunate indeed.

*   *   *

The first woman I met at Notre Dame was named Helen. She reminded me of a Beatles' song; she was sixty-four and losing her hair. For a few weeks, given the male/female ratio at that time, she was my best prospect for a dance date. Today the proper term is "housekeeper," but in the '70s they were still called maids. I get funny looks today when I slip and tell a student to get a broom from the maid's closet. These women (and some men) still vacuum hallway carpets, clean the bathrooms, and haul out the beer cans piled high in corridor trash cans, but they don't clean individual student rooms anymore.

Actually, they didn't do much room cleaning when I was an undergraduate which is probably why many of them were phased out. They were willing, but usually the trash piles were too high for them to work around and too toxic to touch even with rubber gloves. That's another thing that hasn't changed much. They would occasionally scour our room sinks with Comet and make pointed yet accurate remarks about the black film taking life on the ceramic surfaces. Students' sinks are a better argument in support of evolution than most scientific explanations I've heard. Sometimes if they liked us, the maids made our beds, even if that was not part of their job description and landed them in trouble with their supervisors for going above and beyond the call.

I do regret, in the interests of public health, that students now have to bring their own sheets. The University used to provide white ones washed in the laundry service's scalding hot water that shrunk them so the bottom end barely reached the end of the mattress. Black and white signs were posted in the hallways announcing sheet exchange every two weeks between 11:30 AM and 1:30 PM.

The practice encouraged us to believe that changing sheets every couple of weeks was a normal habit, like tooth-brushing and showering. Now, since students must provide their own, no institutional incentive exists to disinfect them, especially since they have to pay for wash in real coin. I know some of their bedding goes the entire semester without a cleaning either because their mother did it for them at home or I'm the only one suggesting it here. I avoid looking too closely when stopping by their rooms.

Some years ago, a student got nicknamed "Goat" after the clothes pile in the corner of his room began to crawl with vermin feeding on the Oreos and Doritos crumbs buried within. We had to intervene when the roommate came to the rector in despair, moaning that he was lying awake at nights terrorized by visions of cockroaches crawling up his legs. Unfortunately, it is not uncommon for undergraduate males to toss food into the corner indiscriminately with the clothes and let it mingle for a month. I don't know where they learned to purchase large bottles of Fabreze as a substitute for doing laundry or housecleaning. It makes the place (and the ones who use it for deodorant) smell a little better, but I don't believe that it helps at all to repel roaches.

Helen retired during my sophomore year, left her position as head of the maid's crew, and was replaced by Skipper, who is still employed on campus in the less strenuous position of checking students into the South Dining Hall. A good chunk of today's housekeepers are from Bosnia, and they have formed quite a strong, if informal, employment network here on campus.

The ones who stay loyally for decades work like dogs, and "administrative efficiencies" imposed in recent years require them to do more with fewer personnel in less time. In administrative and academic buildings, the introduction of those paperless new computer systems causes white-collars to keep piling excessive piles of paper into the wastebaskets the blue-collars are paid far less to lug down stairs. In residence halls where cans and bottles predominate, it is edifying to witness their dedication day in and day out, picking up after college kids who have more disposable income for beer than they have for their own children's Christmas presents. Our students are rarely rude to them on purpose. In fact, they are generally quite respectful and generous each year when we take up the annual housekeeper Christmas collection. It's just that the male species is often oblivious to what pigs (and goats) they can be and how much backbreaking work their normal daily routine creates, particularly in a 120-year-old building without an elevator. Our housekeeper, Senija, always appreciates it when we have a few miscreants lined up to do trash detail, and anyone who's been a rector will tell you that the housekeeper is your closest ally.

Few of ours have calluses in their futures, but I don't begrudge the great-grandchildren of immigrants their future prospects. I do hope they learn that how one treats those below them on the totem pole is a better measurement of their character than how skillful they are at kissing up to their bosses above. Senija, Miss Leitha, and the other housekeepers, like the Helens and Skippers before them, have also humanized and civilized us through successive generations. I hope that we always have them around and strive to be even more grateful for their labor. Many of them last longer than rectors, with far less reward.

CHAPTER 15

ZWISCHENSPIEL
IM OSTERREICH

MY INTERLUDE FROM HALL LIFE was anything but – eight and a half months surrounded by the Austrian Alps and forty undergraduates, thirty-five sophomores, and five juniors during the 1996-97 academic year. I may be the only person who saw The Sound of Music but never wanted to go to Salzburg and listen to music make the hills come alive. The University of Portland, where we also have a large contingent of Holy Cross religious stationed, has sponsored an overseas program there since 1964. When asked previously if I be interested in being its director, I'd always responded, "Why would I want to spend a year in Austria cooped up all alone with forty kids?"

Of course, I did get asked to go, and I went. When I returned to campus the following May, people asked me, "What did you do all year?" "Well," I said, "Imagine yourself as a single parent with forty college kids living under your roof on co-ed floors, 7,000 miles from home in a country where you don't know the language, and the drinking age is sixteen. What *do* you think I did all year long?"

The schedule called for us to meet in London and spend eleven days gradually busing our way through half of Western Europe. The first night I read them the riot act: "Rule number one is trains and planes don't wait, so neither will the bus. If you miss it, make sure you have your passport, a copy of the itinerary, and enough cash to catch up to us." I saw a few mouths hanging open. It was a Sunday night. I was optimistic that the effect of my rant might last a few days.

The next morning they were all there at 8:30 AM, but I could have poured half of them onto the bus. On the way in, I'd noticed a bar called "Filthy McNasty's" a few blocks from the dorm we were booked into. So, apparently, had they. It was a long day of touring for some of them, bouncing along the narrow streets of London, especially for those who combined a tendency toward motion sickness on top of their hangovers and got stuck at the back of our motor coach.

I incurred a few hostile faces the previous afternoon shortly before our meeting as well. I had gone out to meet nineteen of them arriving at Heathrow on the same plane, then escorted them the length of the terminal for their first taste of the London Tube. It would have been easier to herd a flock of water buffalo. Scrambling and stumbling with all their bags, I wasn't sure they all made it onto the subway. However, more than half had already made it on their own to the residence hall where we were staying. So would the stragglers, I told them, although my feigned indifference about whether some had missed the train caused one young traveler to gasp in horror at my callousness.

When we got to King's Cross station, I was pleased to count up all nineteen of them and smiled in the direction of the one who'd worried that I'd left a couple at the airport – and missed the gospel parable about the lost sheep during my theology studies. We should have transferred to another train for one more stop that would have left us with about a half mile to walk; however, that station was closed for maintenance.

I did give them the option of a cab – told them it would be only four or five more dollars per person. It wasn't much considering most of them could drop five times that on ale in an evening without a second thought, but they were husbanding their beer money carefully. Only a few took that option. The rest decided to walk, about ten blocks more after the long haul to the Tube, over uneven gray cobblestones without handicapped curbs. I was honest with them about how long a hike it would be.

They were all laden down with a year's worth of luggage: Samsonite suitcases big as a bulldozer, a backpack half as large, a fanny pack, and in most cases, a couple of other bags. The women who were carting three times their body weight began to melt along with the men who didn't look much better. One stopped dead, halted the entire line behind her, put hands on hips, and glared at me icily. She was just about to declare her refusal to take one more step forward. Then her bargaining power lessened as it began to rain, rather heavily.

Since I did have a free hand, I cheerfully popped open my

umbrella. "It's only five or six more blocks," I said with a wave and kept walking fifty feet ahead at a moderately brisk pace. I had given them the taxi option; it was really not my fault. Still, if my protester had been carrying so much as a butter knife, I'm convinced I would have been chopped up for breakfast bacon right there on the sidewalk. But they did learn to travel light, and no one on that trek packed more than he or she could carry again. Now she's one of my most regular correspondents from the group. I relish receiving regular updates and digital pictures of her growing children.

The next morning I grabbed the bus microphone and woke up those trying to nap. When we were traveling, I often waited until most had fallen asleep, especially if I suspected them of having spent most of the night at a nasty bar, to grab the mike and bellow out, "Attention, attention, how's everyone doing back there? Look out the window and see what beautiful scenery you're missing?"

That first day I just asked how they liked breakfast. There was general muttering at my interruption. Then I said, "You know those sausages that looked like hockey pucks. Anyone have them?" A good number raised their hands. I then added, "Those were *blood* sausages" and sat down to a symphony of disgusting groans. That also wasn't my fault. Though I never admitted it to them, I'd gulped down a couple before I figured out what they were too. I was debating whether to look for a store that sold sick bags. I'd scored one point, but after that it was a slaughter for the other side.

Three nights later, we were due to take off the next morning for France. A fire alarm rang. I almost didn't leave the building since there had been a false alarm the previous night, but I reminded myself that I was supposed to be a role model. When I walked outside, there was a cloud of black smoke billowing from a third floor room. Someone next to me said, "Isn't that Bill and Mike's room?" I checked my room roster and in fact it was. One of them had left an incense stick burning after leaving the room. Somehow it had caught the draperies on fire.

I didn't have any illusions about why a college student might be carting around incense, but my immediate concern was getting out of the country. We were due to leave early the next morning. I wasn't pleased that my first call back to the States was to report that one of our students had almost burned down an eight-story building. I seriously doubted the authorities would allow us to leave England's shores unless I returned from the Bank of London with five thousand pounds I didn't have in my wallet. Luckily, the fire was contained within the room, and the University had enjoyed a long relationship with their overseas counterparts. Still, I didn't breathe evenly until we'd gotten ashore across the English Channel the next afternoon. Vive la France! I was wondering if I could get away with ditching them all and enjoying Paris on my own. It was just the first week.

*   *   *

Six days later I did learn something essential about the differences between men and women. We were a day away from reaching Salzburg and conducted room picks out of a hat in a gasthaus in Ruette, one of those charming postcard towns surrounded by Alps in Western Austria. Downstairs was a combined restaurant and bar, though by the time we got to picking rooms, only the bar part was still functioning. Sixteen men picked rooms. When they found out who their roommates were, they uniformly said to each other something like, "Great, let's go have another beer." They would solve their differences later in the year the easy way – by brawling.

Twenty-four women then picked. I had told both sexes, "You can switch if you want, but you have to talk to the person you don't want to room with about why before coming to me." I didn't want to start off the year with any undercurrents of resentment. I gave them an hour and went to my room. With the door open, I listened as small groups went up and down the hallways. I peeked out occasionally and saw small conclaves with shifting membership being held in whispers on the stairs.

An hour and a half later, a delegation of five came to me with a list. They'd made thirteen changes and assured me their arrangements would work out better. They hadn't followed my guidelines, however, so I paused to think. A little voice in my head said, "Do what they say, or your life is going to be a living hell for the next eight months," so I capitulated. I didn't have a serious roommate issue all year. It was one of the few things I didn't get blamed for. All of a sudden it made sense why men don't like to stand next to one another at urinals and women always go to the john in twos.

Whenever we had to put on a big dinner or something of the sort later in the year, I never put a man in charge if I could avoid it. Early on I found myself facing a social disaster when the male who was supposedly in charge decided to leave town the night before a large contingent of University guests were due to arrive. Sure enough, a team of women spontaneously banded together to rescue me as if I were an abandoned puppy showing up on the threshold in the midst of a Christmas blizzard. They cooked food, baked desserts, mopped the floor, and got everything from drinks to doilies put out on time. I bought them flowers afterward. I got a lot smarter that year, but it was a process.

A few weeks after we arrived, one of the girls came to me in tears because she had damaged a car parked on the street while throwing a ball around. I was quite aware that not all the neighbors relished having forty boisterous nineteen- and twenty-year-old Americans living next across from them on Merianstrasse Street, so I went down to take a look. It was just a cracked sideview mirror. I didn't get upset or yell. I told her matter of factly, "It's not that big a deal. Just leave a note on the windshield with your name. Apologize and say you'll be glad to pay for it." Then I started walking away, thinking I had done well to remain calm and succeeded at providing comfort. I couldn't understand why she was silently shooting daggers at me. Only later did I grasp what she really wanted was a hug, not a solution.

One night weeks later, a guy came into my room and asked if I had any aspirin. I had my back to him, pointed to the cabinet on the wall, and went back to typing. He grunted "Thanks" and walked out. A couple of days later, one of the ladies walked in, asked if I had any Tylenol, and I did the same. Two days later one of her friends walked into the office, stood over me threateningly and shouted, "I have a bone to pick with you." I knew I was about to get body-slammed. "She came in here to talk with you, and you didn't pay any attention to her. She *needed* to talk with you, and you ignored her. She's having major problems, and you don't even care!" It took a while for the brain to unfog and realize that's what the other one meant when she said she wanted Tylenol. I changed.

From that point onward, whenever a woman came to see me, I turned around in my chair, adopted a pose that signaled I was really interested in whatever she had to say, and set aside the next fifteen minutes to chatting. Usually nothing else followed. To me it was wasting time when I had work to do. To them it was bonding emotionally with their director. I had never realized women don't make friends by putting on gloves and breaking one another's noses.

I learned more about the two planets' orbits that year than the rest of my life combined. I have some confidence that husbands, mothers, and female rectors too will sympathize at least a bit, though a friend of mine told me after reading the first draft of this that I needed a sister growing up! I suppose he's right, but I have made progress. Come to think of it, I might not make such a bad rector for the Pangborn Hall Phoxes someday – once I get tired of picking up dirty boxers in the Sorin bathrooms.

*   *   *

After we'd been in Salzburg for a week, we had a formal beginning of the year dinner with the faculty, staff, and spouses in a fancy lodge on the outskirts of town. On the bus ride over, the driver, who was also our landlord and travel agent, told me to get on the mike and announce to the group that the drinks were free. I stared incredulously and said, "What?!" He repeated, "Tell them it is an open bar." Not knowing any better, I did to stirring applause from forty college kids who were thrilled their director had flipped in the very first month.

Three and a half hours later, there was a conga line throwing up in the bushes. I had spotted some of them doing shots of schnapps with faculty and staff enablers fifteen minutes before. It was only at that point that Gerhard came up and dryly informed me, "You can close the bar anytime." They got along very well with Gerhard that year. The next week I got a bill for $2,200. I noticed that the previous year's dinner had cost $1,500. I decided not to call that in to the bosses back at the ranch in Oregon. Score a three-pointer for them.

A couple weeks later they decided to go to Oktoberfest. I was glad all forty were heading up to Munich together. I told them to just make sure everyone got home. I didn't need to know the details. Later in the year I did hear about the fights, a chase, and a couple who needed to be carried to the train like limp sacks of garbage, but at the end of the day, I said to myself, "It's a victory if they all make it to the end." That's when I adopted my not-so-minimal definition of a successful year in a student residence hall.

Then the first week in October the officers and a good number of board members from the University showed up to dedicate our new center. By midnight, they had disappeared, but several of our Austrian faculty members stuck around to demonstrate their solidarity by dancing on tables with the students. The political science professor had to be driven home by a sophomore shortly after 2:00 AM. In the United States, we call those boundary issues.

I'd hired him several weeks before when his predecessor told me that she would not be finishing the semester. She had been unexpectedly offered a plum job working for the government in Vienna. I thought I had a couple of weeks to scramble for a replacement; however, to my surprise, Sandra showed up two days later, fifteen minutes before the next class started with her replacement in tow. She hadn't cleared it with me. I was informed – politely but firmly – that she was going to walk downstairs, say a few words about the Austrian government's structure, bid farewell to our group, and then turn over the class to him.

I'd been in the country barely a week but quickly found out they did things differently in Austria. Usually, a program director interviews prospective faculty before hiring them, but it was awfully hard under the circumstances to refuse his services. I promptly drew up the contract. However, three weeks later, after my newest faculty role model had been carted home like a teenage Oktoberfest reveler, I doubted whether I would ever regain the upper hand over my Salzburg group.

However, as the year progressed, I generally knew more than they thought I did and usually refrained from commenting immediately. Many of them developed an obsession about playing Spades in the common room. I like cards, not really enough to play every day, but by positioning myself against the back wall like a wary Mafia don, I could watch everyone coming in and out the front door which told me a lot about who was up to what without looking like I was spying. It was the Austrian equivalent of crosswords on the porch.

Following upon the "Presence Prevents Problems" principle, I realized that merely sitting there was a deterrent and gave them a security blanket they didn't always want to admit they needed. It also gave me some semblance of control over the immediate environment, if not what they did on weekend excursions to Amsterdam. They might get into trouble elsewhere, but they never quite knew whether they would run into me coming home at night after cavorting in town. I got pretty good at Spades too, though I didn't play again for ten years.

For Christmas they decided to produce a video to send home to their parents. I was hesitant about would kind of MPAA rating the content would get. Some had more liberal parents than others, and they wanted me to participate. I decided that I'd better be proactive and stage my own role in the filming. One of them came into my office with a video camera. I greeted the folks and deadpanned about how everything was going smoothly with no problems of any sort. Their children were well-supervised and acting in perfect order, just like I was the Colonel with the whistle and they were the Von Trapp kids before Maria showed up and started dressing them up in draperies.

Meanwhile, I positioned them on the balcony behind me where they were having a water fight, hoisting beer bottles, and pitching stuff down into the courtyard below with my back to them the entire time, pretending to be oblivious. I figured if the parents thought their kids were only joking, they would be reassured. It was akin to an inoculation: give them a little fake chaos so they wouldn't stop to consider what might actually be going on over there.

Luckily, that was eleven years ago, before cell phones. I didn't even have an answering machine, and the push-button phone was in the office thirty feet from my bedroom, so I couldn't hear it at night. I got a few calls from parents, but I know a director couldn't get away without being glued to a cell now. It's a consideration in thinking about whether I'd ever go back and listen to the hills echoing again.

*   *   *

The first momentous holiday of the year was Halloween a couple of weeks after filming. They scheduled a house party. I had told them I was not dressing up; I cringe at the very thought of Halloween. An hour before the party was started I found myself looking at a vase filled with dried stalks and had an inspiration. I took them back to my room, borrowed a t-shirt with a pocket, put on a pair of jeans, grabbed an empty beer bottle, wrapped a bandanna around my head and stuck the stalks under it to resemble cornrows. After the party started I walked over, staggered in like I was loaded, and pretended to be spitting tobacco juice into the bottle.

They awarded me first prize in the costume contest for dressing like Andy who was quite surprised to encounter his double on the stairs, though he failed to grasp the hints I was attempting to drop through mockery about his appearance and behavior. The other problem was that several of them took pictures while I was in costume acting like him. Some of them still have those pictures. It was a pretty good acting job; no one looking at them now would ever believe I was dead sober.

But by the end of spring break in March, I was shot. My bag of tricks was empty, and they knew it was too late in the year to be sent home for anything less than a felony arrest. I had just returned from a three-week tour of Greece and Italy with them. Venice came at the end of the trip. Most people love Venice, but I didn't care for it at all. The food was expensive, and the canals stunk like sewer water. I prefer walking streets to paying the cost of a good pair of Italian shoes for a thirty-minute gondola ride. The people in St. Mark's Square encouraging pigeons to land on their shoulders were revolting. I just wanted to go home.

Then a little more than a month later, we held an optional second retreat. I was surprised that we had gotten 100 percent participation for the first one back in October. I was shocked when, after eight months of living on a little American island in the midst of frowning, lederhosen-bedecked burghers, all forty of them chose to do another together instead of jaunting off to EuroDisneyland. They ended it by going around in a circle with everyone standing face to face saying what they liked and appreciated about each other, then hugging. I tried to escape, but they made me join in. It was corny. It also took two and half hours. Several boys and a few more girls left salt stains on my shoulder.

At first, I felt like I had descended into Purgatory early. I kept looking at my watch wondering whether Johann, our bus driver, bored while burning through a pack of Marlboros outside, would give up and abandon us. Then I got a little schmaltzy too. They'd all navigated the odds successfully despite fire and foe – and, even more amazingly, eight couples dating in the house at the same time. That year was a lifeboat experience.

I was a third of the way across the world with no health services, discipline officers, counselors, security force, residence life staff, or even a single RA to be my eyes and ears. We had a cook/housefrau who acted like she was the head matron at the Bastille and terrorized me daily along with a landlord who loved to see bars opened but not closed. Fortunately, the gooey retreat helped me to recover from the spring break trip. I finally spotted a flicker of light at the top of the salt mine and realized that I wouldn't end my days in an Austrian asylum begging for scraps of day-old apfelstrudel after all.

I should have been forewarned when I traveled over the previous March to see what I was in for and sat across from my predecessor for six uninterrupted hours watching his hands tremble as he rambled on about his group's infantile exploits. Mine came close on a few occasions to sending me around the bend, though by the end of the year they were telling me more than I wanted to know, not to mention sharing incriminating pictures of their travels with me.

I adapted to bossy Austrians, women screaming at me, men casually abandoning their leader, and days feeling overwhelmed, like the boy with his finger in the dike hole, but the program changed even more after I left the position. The University later hired a local assistant director to help out and be a second pair of eyes; conducted a normal job search for another political science prof; made its students learn more German than "eins, zwei, drei" before leaving the States; and cut out the eleven-day boozing bus cruise that used to inaugurate the year in London.

It was the most challenging thing I've ever done and without a doubt the most rewarding. There isn't a group of students I will ever feel closer to or one for which I will do a larger proportion of weddings, including Andy's, the guy with the cornrows and bandanna. Last Christmas he sent me a picture with his wife and daughter under which was written, "Thanks for providing the sacrament." Well, it was grace for me too. Every week I got to watch two-thirds on average and sometimes more, show up for Sunday night Mass – even if the piano player hit a few wrong notes after doing the local brewery tour earlier in the day. They certainly provided me with my ultimate lesson in patience.

In an ideal world, we would all prefer that sophomores not pass out under German beer tents, but the sacramental part from my perspective was watching how those forty cooped up kids cared for one another until the end, sometimes quite touchingly. They had a similar attitude to the Marines: leave no man or woman behind. It's the bottom line I draw in the sand and insist Otters abide by when they've blown off all other advice, warnings, and printed commandments.

There were factions, jealousies, and arguments, of course, but a Salzburger could always find a traveling partner. Those who weren't best friends with another would nevertheless make sure that the one on the verge of being left out was included somehow. It wasn't always a joyride, but people weren't ostracized, ignored, or ditched if they wanted to tag along. Like Ed Mack tells his O'Neill freshmen during Orientation Weekend, "Everyone has a place at the table," no matter how they may be different.

Whether at Portland or Notre Dame, we aim for a spiritual communion among our students which is a higher ideal than celebrating diversity. This group instinctively grasped that aspiration, and it became not only my goal but theirs to make it as one to the end. There were some close calls, but, in fact, that was one of the few years someone hadn't left the program for personal, academic, medical, or disciplinary reasons – though in the latter category I think I could have made a few charges stick.

Occasionally, I've been tempted to return to that job, although it might be more entertaining to wait about fifteen years until their kids start showing up in the program. I do have a small bit of regret that with the program changes, I couldn't repeat the walk from King's Cross station. I've picked up a few more tricks in the decade since. Now I know that on foreign soil I wouldn't need to worry about American privacy laws, and I'd search every piece of overgrown Samsonite for incense sticks once I dragged them all in out of the rain.

CHAPTER 16

S–s–w–e–e–t!

I HAVE TO BE CAREFUL not to pull rector pranks too often. Almost seven years to the day after my last film acting job in the Christmas video, my first Sorin College staff asked me to tape a spot for our talent show scheduled for Halloween weekend. Still glowing from my earlier success in the Salzburg costume contest, I thought I'd throw a bone to the troops, so I put on a black cape, greased my hair back, and did what I thought was a standard Bela Lugosi routine. I kept repeating "Come here" in a Transylvanian accent with my right hand extended into a claw, just like he did in the old *Dracula* movie, while walking toward the camera.

It was the first time I'd dressed up since my year abroad (and the last). I was brimming with confidence, but for some reason, it didn't go over quite so well. Most who watched it said it was "freaky." It's also possible fewer of them have abandoned their X-Boxes long enough to watch Bela in a 1931 black and white classic and just don't get how good my imitation was. Like with tackle football in the snow, I may have reached the point where

219

retirement is the best option even when they egg me on to do otherwise. Or maybe Portland students just have a better sense of humor.

I do give myself credit for not succumbing to temptations that have waylaid other rectors. My one fundamental rule is that I have never done anything that cannot be undone within five minutes. I have never shaved my head or beard, or gotten a Mohawk. A couple of less prudent rectors in recent memory have emulated then-Father Jenky's example and been baited into altering their appearance when their halls hit a charity goal or won an interhall sports championship.

Several years ago, one of our younger priests walked into the Corby Hall social hour and turned a few of the elder fathers' heads by arriving with carnation pink hair after losing a bet with his guys. Even I, who knew him to be stable, almost spilled my martini onto the floor in astonishment. I've kept the pictures too. I'm just waiting for the right moment to display them in front of a crowd unaware of his past folly.

Some rectors with more sense than me have donned costumes into their '60s. For almost twenty years, Father George wore a white tux with green tie and cummerbund and lay in a coffin during Alumni Hall's annual signature event, the Wake. Then the law in Student Affairs clamped down on that tradition too. Maybe it isn't such a hot idea for a rector to be de facto out of commission for an hour on a big weekend night, but George did make a resplendent corpse.

He still roasts all the graduating seniors at year's end, however, and the Dawgs look forward with keen anticipation to discovering how much he really knew all year that he didn't let on to. Of course, he also solicits contributions from those anxious to rat out their brothers in the name of good entertainment. After thirty years, they've learned that they can trust him not to be vengeful about crimes committed earlier in the year. There is an unofficial statute of limitations for most antics.

I did something like that for a couple of years. One Otter had a potty mouth that could be heard two floors away at the opposite end of the building. It was most noticeable when he screamed at the TV screen while playing Halo video games. I gave him a dog muzzle as a Christmas present in front of the entire hall, and it did no good at all. In his third year, he went overseas for a semester.

I don't know if he got culture in Europe or just got bored with Halo, but he seemed to return a bit quieter. Mike was a tough kid. I could mess with him without worrying that his feelings would get bruised, but sometimes they are more sensitive than they look. I do discriminate and try to pick only on the ones who can handle it.

I don't quite think I'm ready to give up on the occasional prank though. After all, I live with people who have been known to keep snakes as roommates. I had a neighbor across the hall in a Dillon single in 1988-89 who always slipped in and out quickly and locked the door behind him. He rarely entertained visitors, but since he never got into any trouble either, I didn't pry. I don't like to be nosy without cause. However, I was a bit disturbed that May. One of the last remaining freshmen at year's end let slip that the guy had been housing a python most of the year in a cardboard box. I don't like snakes. I was a chicken as a kid, afraid even of worms until sixth grade.

I was especially displeased to be told of the night that I was napping on the couch with my head just a couple of feet from the door when the hungry creature escaped from his box and had slithered halfway across the hallway before being snatched up. When I live with people who let reptiles slither around dangerously close to my earlobe in the place I call home, I do not endure many Catholic guilt pangs about the occasional, harmless payback.

*   *   *

Sometimes we also have the opportunity to provide one and demonstrate that we're not as dumb as we look just because we look ancient to them. Mr. Ed Mack, who has now served joyfully for six years in O'Neill, is not a C.S.C.; however, he did spend twenty-four years teaching at one of our high schools and might as well be one of us. I'm glad that maintenance personnel, UPS drivers, alumni, and other visitors assume he's a priest and inevitably call him "Father." It connotes an expectation and assumption that people hold about Holy Cross' commitment to residential life. I'm pleased he always laughs and doesn't mind being lumped in with us too.

One night during his first year, an O'Neill RA informed us that a group of third-floor sophomores and juniors were planning a "Night of Two Thousand Beers." It was to be a belated Y2K celebration. We debated what to do. We had no hard evidence that eighty cases of beer had been carted into the building. If they had, we weren't sure which rooms to look in. A full-scale search of the entire wing could have led to the first good riot in almost twenty years, especially if we came up empty-handed. You never want to go hunting if you're not sure of bagging your quarry, and no new rector wants a full-scale rebellion on his first end-of-the-year performance review.

We could have threatened them, but we didn't want to just wag our finger ninny-like and say, "Don't you dare!" We pondered the dilemma for a while and hit upon a novel approach. Rather than cutting off the supply, we'd artificially deflate the demand curve. We'd taken economics too. We didn't say anything to them, but when the evening started, we stationed a staff member at each end of the corridor. We only let a few people through at a time so that no crowd ever materialized. Most gave up and walked off in search of other party venues. Ed just sat in the third floor lounge for four hours cheerfully reading a book and occasionally waving at passersby.

The sponsors were sputtering with frustration. Periodically, they would come out to glare at him, but they couldn't move the stash out of the section because we guarded both exits. They couldn't very well complain either. That would have meant admitting they had stockpiled a large supply of illegal goods. What does a frustrated party thrower do? Walk up to your rector and say, "Why aren't you letting hundreds of people into our hallway to drink two thousand beers we stuck into gym bags and smuggled in under your nose?"

Besides, we didn't tell them they couldn't have people over. We were doing them a favor by limiting the crowds. If we'd let it go forward unimpeded, inevitably some would have gotten in serious trouble. We had their best interests at heart. We allow social gatherings but not parties. We were merely exerting our educational responsibilities in teaching them the subtle difference between how to act in our house as opposed to *Animal House*.

*　　　　*　　　　*

For several years before my arrival in Sorin, the highlight of our talent show was the Milk Chug. Upperclassmen, typically sophomores who had attempted the feat the year before, recruited six to eight freshmen to stand in front of the stage before the crowd at the event's conclusion and try to drink a gallon of whole milk. There was a reason why they placed large garbage cans alongside.

I was taken by surprise my first year and afterward struggled to figure out how to quash it without engineering my own revolt. They acted like the chugging milk was as sacred a ritual as singing the alma mater at game's end. I figured it must have been going on for thirty years. Luckily, the next year it poured and there was no show. The following week they ordered the stage and sound equipment to try once more. Again angels in heaven cried buckets in answer to a rector's prayer. I spotted a group that went out anyway with gallons of milk, but there were no spectators, and any evidence quickly washed away.

The next year I was prepared. Again, instead of launching a frontal assault, I decided to put my economics training to practical use but this time by targeting the supply curve. I went out to the supermarket and bought eight quarts of skim, handed them to the assistant rector standing next to the stage, and spread the word that the milkman had already made his delivery. I thought we were safe, but just before the end of the show, I was standing out front and noticed some whispering taking place on stage among the usual suspects who then went back into the hall through the front door.

I knew the game was up, so I ran around the back of the building and raced down the first floor hallway just in time to see several carting out gallons of whole milk. I stopped them and said, "Hold on. I'm buying your milk." I handed one of them a $20 to ease the pain and locked the gallons of whole in my office. I've never forgotten an important lesson from Hannibal that I first learned in a high school ancient history class: speed and surprise in warfare usually wins the day over superior numbers. I'm glad that I've continued reading military history as a hobby for the last thirty years. It's proven to be excellent preparation for rectoring.

Then I stood inside the doorway behind the stage and listened to Alec, our emcee, announce the "highlight" of the Talent Show, the annual milk chug. Six freshmen stepped out, and our assistant rector handed them the quarts of skim. They all got their fill without depositing any contributions into the garbage cans, then looked around with the rest of the Otters wondering where the remaining moo juice was. The show ended with confusion on everyone's faces. Did someone not buy enough milk? What happened?

I suppose they had a clue when they all filed in and saw me standing in the lobby wearing a grin I simply could not wipe away. After a few minutes, they figured out that they had been outflanked by an amateur economist. Some were mad, and I suppose a few of the more sophomoric ones clung to their resentments for a while because I had destroyed their most cherished tradition. However, I hadn't told them they couldn't have a milk chug, and, in fact, they did have one, sort of. I had just outsmarted them, and while they were frustrated, I like to imagine that they secretly have admired their old poop of a rector for proving that he wasn't the dullest knife in the drawer after all.

Some day they might also realize that puking on guests' feet in the middle of a football weekend is a good way to stimulate the kind of outraged complaint letters to people with Dome offices that insure even venerable traditions like the "119th annual Sorin Talent Show" don't see a 120th incarnation. Even if they didn't appreciate it, I had their backs. Later I found out that the "tradition" was only three years old when I arrived. My biggest laugh is going to come the day that I hold this book up and watch their faces when I reveal that it's mostly about them. Sometimes they walk in and ask things like, "What do you do all day?" They think everything works spontaneously around here by automatic pilot.

I can tell that some have been getting suspicious about why I've been spending so much time lately on my computer, though few have said anything to me directly. Alec, the jocular emcee, even walked in one day and told me that I should write a book while I was sitting in my recliner editing some chapters. So did the father of one of the thieves from Chapter Four, but no one's guessed. The payback will be sweet when

I wave the finished product under their noses. Every rector deserves to score a three-pointer once in awhile too.

*   *   *

A college friend of mine's dad was an undergraduate in the late '50s. He didn't like the idea of lights out at eleven, so he tapped into the electrical system in order to be able to read late at night. He managed to keep it secret until one night in late January when the jerry-rigged wires shorted out and set the room afire.

After he had succeeded in charring most of the room like a Texas steak, the disciplinary honchos of that era decided to expel him. He appealed to the president. Luckily, he had been Father Hesburgh's altar server for his daily Mass in the crypt below the Basilica.

Father Ted commuted the sentence and let him stay at Notre Dame. He also graciously allowed him to remain in his dorm room in Lyons, but he ordered the maintenance department not to make even the most minor repair until the end of the semester. It was a very cold winter.

*   *   *

My favorite hall sport is Dollar Derby. I got in trouble one night for it. I was among the crowd in the hallway watching after quiet hours, about 12:35 AM, when one of my assistant rectors came out of his room to tell everyone to knock it off. The comment from the peanut in the gallery was, "Father Jim's here, so it's OK." I don't think it compromised his long-term authority. He lasted another full year, but I do feel guilty whenever I am the cause of staff dissonance, even in a small matter.

As an old, historic building, we have open stairwells from

227

the basement all the way up to the third floor. The upward draft resulting from this design feature makes me pray regularly that someone with the post-party munchies does not pass out while heating up frozen burritos in the oven at 5:30 AM and set the building ablaze. It also allows someone to drop a dollar bill from the third floor and watch an especially nimble young Otter race down the stairs three or four at a time and catch it in the basement before it hits the carpet. It is truly tragic when he reaches the bottom in time but muffs the catch, and I join roundly in the hooting that follows.

They should probably use a ten or twenty for all the trouble and risk, but the opportunity to make their mark in the hall annals matters more than the prospect of increasing their personal net assets. I know one of them may smash their face bones one day stumbling down after a buck, but I just can't bring myself to bring the hammer down on it.

Unfortunately, we do live in an age where college students have to sign legal waivers to cook burgers on the grill in their front yard. Educational institutions are driven by paranoia and intimidated by parents who have lawyers on speed dial, even more so this year with questions about what we're doing to prevent on-campus shootings. It's a long way from a backyard in Canaryville when we were ten years old and put on boxing gloves in backyards without any adults feeling compelled to hang around and referee.

It's like telling younger kids they can't jump off dirt hills with their bikes. Ours could get hit by a snowplow cruising through campus in a blizzard or crack open their spines in a sanctioned interhall basketball game too even when they've signed four waivers. Anyone who tried to repeat Father Ted's solution to a student room torching his room would probably be raked over the coals in a 60 Minutes exposé for excessive cruelty. However, the accidental arsonist (and his parents) appreciated the justice of the sentence, and there are more serious dangers to fret about than eighteen year olds chasing down stairs after floating dollars.

I'm getting weary of students coming into my room to ask whether they can do something relatively harmless and responding, "You have to fill out a form . When the Harry Potterish ones want to color outside the lines, I do my best to avoid dumping mounds of permission slips upon them. I understand one of the reasons why kids like the books. The better teaching wizards are surrogate parents in the mold of Atticus Finch. They know most of what the Hogwarts students are up to but use wands upon them sparingly. A litigious, risk-fearing culture that equates wisdom with credentials and supervision with procedure is increasingly at odds with our sensible pastoral philosophy. Father Moreau said we should try "treating them with the indulgence that their age deserves while distinguishing slight faults from those that reflect malice and dangerous tendencies." It's the handful of Malfoys we should be tying up in knots.

It is also healthy for adults to recognize the difference between having some good reasons to be paranoid and constantly indulging paranoia. My staff that wrote the letter about how I listened to them some of the time was right. It is the big picture that really matters.

CHAPTER 17

THE HEARTBEAT
OF NOTRE DAME

TWENTY YEARS AGO I claimed in my final theology degree project that our residence hall ministry at Notre Dame was rooted implicitly in the scriptural model of Jesus as Good Shepherd. Like the Lord, our first purpose is to know each student by name, just like Father George knew mine before he ever popped up from behind his card table to greet me. Every July when I begin making flash cards of freshman pictures and names, I stop to wonder whether I wasn't quite as dumb in my twenties as I used to think.

We may not understand all of them as much as we'd like, but Notre Dame rectors certainly know our students and what they are up to more than the twenty-four-year-old graduate student directors in charge of residence halls at our counterpart institutions. All I can say to parents is that if your heart is palpitating about Dollar Derby, just pause to imagine the daily chaos engulfing co-ed floors in twelve-story high-rises at Columbus or Madison.

J.E. (Joseph E.) Cusack was the name of the first student to move into Sorin on January 1, 1889. He graduated that June, so his tenure was brief. The oral tradition is that he was awarded the first room pick because of his academic prowess. It may not have hurt his popularity that he was also the starting left half-back on Notre Dame's first football squad which had played its first game against Michigan two seasons earlier. The hall study lounge right across from our main entrance is named after him. On the wall next to the door hang two pictures of Cusack, one in his football uniform and the other in a graduation tuxedo, the first in a long line of student-athletes.

Four years earlier, when Cusack first rode up the main drive, literally under one-horse power, he would have headed for the not quite completed Main Building still waiting for the statue of the Virgin Mary that crowns it today. After the previous structure housing most of the University had burned to the ground in April 1879, the present one was thrown up by more than three hundred laborers working eighteen-hour days throughout the summer. The plaster was still drying in September as furniture was being carted in, but the building was in decent enough shape for classes to start and students to be housed in barrack-like quarters by the first day of the term.

Knute Rockne may have given the most famous pep talk in Notre Dame history, but the most important was given by a sixty-five-year-old Holy Cross priest returning to campus just after the fire. After surveying the damage, Father Sorin gathered the dispirited community of priests and brothers, faculty and staff,

232

religious sisters, students, and friends from town into Sacred Heart Church, a towering French Gothic structure still in progress eight years after the laying of its cornerstone.

They all expected Sorin, who had rushed back from Montreal, to announce the abandonment of the entire enterprise. Notre Dame had survived cholera epidemics, Civil War divisions, perpetual threats of bankruptcy, and several less catastrophic fires, but virtually *everything* had been consumed in this last blaze: classrooms, laboratories, scientific collections, offices, library, and dorm space. Instead, as T.E. Howard later recounted:

> *I was then present when Father Sorin, after looking over the destruction of his life-work, stood at the altar steps of the only building left and spoke to the community what I have always felt to be the most sublime words I ever listened to. There was absolute faith, confidence, resolution in his very look and pose. "If it were ALL gone, I should not give up!" were his words in closing. The effect was electric. It was the crowning moment of his life. A sad company had gone into the church that day. They were all simple Christian heroes as they came out. There was never more a shadow of a doubt as to the future of Notre Dame.*

Just about anyplace else, that account would be dismissed as pure corn, but what is it the fight song says? "What though the odds be great or small . . . ?" I like to imagine the frenzied assembly bursting through out the church doors just as the movie, *Knute Rockne, All-American,* depicts the squad leaving the locker room after the Rock's legendary "Win one for the Gipper" speech – stacking bricks without bothering to exchange cassocks for overalls. In reality, they waited three days for the heap to cool, and it was a group of students along with a Latin professor who wheeled the first barrow.

When classes resumed in the new Main Building the following September, only 324 students had enrolled for the fall semester. The fire had dampened the numbers, and Notre Dame was still a provincial backwater pretending to be a university. Many of its students were still "minims" or grade school boarders. Nevertheless, paltry as its accomplishments were in comparison even to many Midwestern colleges, Sorin had carved a Catholic symbol of pride and hope to immigrant aspirations that towered above miles of Hoosier prairie. In the decade after the fire, the University roared back.

Since his arrival on November 26, 1842 with seven Holy Cross brothers, one mangy ox with wagon, and about $300 cash, the founder had earned the respect not only of the Catholic hierarchy who gathered to concelebrate his Jubilee Mass at Notre Dame on May 27, 1888.but other distinguished Americans as well. Gen. William Tecumseh Sherman's children boarded at Notre Dame during the great sectional conflict, and the stern war hero gave a Commencement address in 1865 in which he urged graduates to "Perform bravely the battle of life."

Senator Henry Clay helped Sorin and his scraggly band of brothers and priests to establish a post office at Notre Dame in 1849, a mere seven years after its founding. Its financial situation was so dire then that pigs and grain were regularly accepted in lieu of tuition. Exhaustive research by others has failed to unearth any sensible reason why the Baptist congressional patriarch from Kentucky agreed to provide such bountiful assistance to Hoosier Catholics. A post office meant a spot on the official U.S. map and was highly prized since roads and rail lines tended to follow.

Even at the peak of anti-Catholic sentiment in the 1850s, the priest with the funny French accent had proven to be a master at marshaling critical support from mission societies, wartime heroes, Catholic bishops, and influential politicians. It was only appropriate that at the sunset of his life the new residence hall with fifty private rooms, gas heat, and individual sinks should be named for him. When the cornerstone was blessed on the very day of his jubilee Mass, it was christened Collegiate Hall, but shortly after the grand celebration, a consensus quickly formed to substitute his name.

It would never have been constructed at all had Sorin not threatened to resign over what most thought was a foolish pipedream. Private rooms for students! What was the need? And the cost! Yet, Sorin insisted that if Notre Dame aspired to be a serious educational institution, its student-scholars required suitable quarters for living and studying, and J.E. Cusack became the first Notre Dame student to benefit from Sorin's foresight. Perhaps more importantly, nearly 120 years later, we haven't forgotten his name either.

*   *   *

At the beginning of each academic year, Father Poorman gives a talk to incoming freshmen and parents about "residentiality," a word which has been used at Notre Dame long before "blog" but will never make it into *Webster's*. As it sounds more like a city planner's term for urban redevelopment, its utility for describing to the uninitiated the philosophy which governs Notre Dame's residence halls is questionable.

However, it connotes the pastoral approach to education specific to the Congregation of Holy Cross that was a dramatic departure from the French boarding school model of the early nineteenth century which favored stern taskmasters armed with horsewhips. If we use the phrase "Notre Dame Family" quite liberally today to express the loyalty engendered here, it is largely because Father Moreau insisted that the young Sorin and others like him educate students during the daytime but also care for them on their own turf, living side by side with them once the formal lessons were over.

As Moreau wrote, "We shall always place education side by side with instruction. The mind will not be cultivated at the expense of the heart. While we prepare useful citizens for society, we shall likewise do our utmost to prepare citizens for eternal life." The distinguishing feature of a Notre Dame education is a commitment to helping students to reach their full potential and nurturing those possibilities at all levels of this institution. The sense of community that envelops this campus has been formed and persistently grounded in that charism, even if we have not always done a very good job of articulating it to our students, alumni, faculty, or staff. Hopefully, Moreau's beatification will spur more of our constituents to search out the pearls in *Christian Education*.

Those ideals of Holy Cross' founder have infused the University's approach to virtually every facet of campus life: its attitudes toward intellectual and spiritual formation; its commitment to fostering service to the less fortunate; our alcohol policies and disciplinary procedures; the placement of religious and clergy in residence halls; its treatment of athletic department issues; and even our relatively lenient attitudes toward the "borrowing" of their sacred gold football helmets.

Not just Sorin College, but every hall also has a unique character, history, nickname, and rector. It is virtually an archaic title outside of Catholic seminaries, British-influenced universities, and Notre Dame, but the rector is the capstone in the arch of the University's philosophy of residentiality. In contrast to the standard logic of management flow charts, rectors still formally report directly to the Vice President of Student Affairs, despite a couple of administrative layers in between. Inevitably, upon being introduced, two or more Irish alumni will ask one another, "What hall were you in?" It doesn't take long before they begin trading their favorite rector stories, and it is not at all unusual to encounter graying parents of current students wandering around campus asking strangers if they know where "my rector" can be found.

On that New Year's Day in 1889 when Cusack moved his steamer trunk into Sorin, he would have quickly encountered Rev. Andrew Morrissey, C.S.C., the first rector of Sorin, striding around its gleaming hallways. Morrissey quickly moved upward and became the University's seventh president in 1893.

He gloomily predicted that Notre Dame was destined to remain little more than a glorified boarding school because "We can never compete with those colleges that have such tremendous endowments."

A succession of other priests and brothers followed Morrissey in Sorin, most serving not more than one or two years as rector. In those days, with fewer dorms, more Holy Cross religious, a number of bachelor dons in residence, far less litigation, and no counseling center, the administrative duties could be shared rather informally among a constantly rotating crew.

One early exception was Rev. John (Pop) Farley, C.S.C.,who became known as the "rector of rectors." An award in his honor is presented annually to a staff member who has contributed significantly to the University's residential mission. Farley was a combination of Bing Crosby in *Going My Way* and present head football coach, Charlie Weis. Genial and big-hearted, sometimes crusty and sarcastic – or perhaps just think of a blockier, more athletic version of *MASH's* Colonel Potter.

He was known as the "snake-whipping, rump-kicking king," a moniker which, hopefully, had more pizzazz in the 1930s. One of his chief delights was in tossing the daily mail from the top step of the Sorin porch to waiting residents along with gratuitous musings about the senders' personal characteristics. He especially enjoyed delivering perfumed missives from "hometown honies," who had no idea a priest would be scrutinizing their mail before handing it over – in a crowd – to their red-faced beaus. We use more indirect means today, some of the time.

Hanging outside my door is a picture of Pop Farley looking a mite older than I, wearing a full religious habit and throwing a baseball over at the old baseball diamond where the Hesburgh Library now stands. He served as the rector of Sorin for eight years beginning in 1930, also Knute Rockne's last season as football coach before his fatal plane crash. I have to admit that after reading some archival material about him, it wasn't too much of a stretch for me to borrow elements of his management style.

I've always been a little "old school" long before it became the name of a raunchy movie. I sometimes think if I'd been born about fifty years early with a few different chromosomes, I could have been a habit-wearing nun happily swashbuckling my way through the hallways with a steel ruler. I like showing that side of myself the first couple of days. Some eighteen year olds you can scare into sobriety – for about a week maybe.

*　　　　*　　　　*

Hopefully, this book captures something of the Notre Dame mystique although it hasn't dealt much with either athletics or academics even though the University ranks near the top in both categories. There are plenty of football books, and besides, after forty years of screaming myself hoarse like a maniacal freshman, I still have trouble recognizing a nickel defense. As for academics, I'm only returning to the classroom for the first time in fifteen years soon after these pages hit the shelves. I have been observing their study habits for a while, but I have typically only read a few papers a year brought to me by those desperate for help.

I do fret sometimes about where we are heading institutionally as our academic ambitions continue to expand. Mae West, the old burlesque queen who was jailed briefly for a risqué Broadway act that would be primetime viewing today, once notably quipped, "I used to be Snow White, but I drifted." It is one of my favorite theological insights, if from a quite unorthodox source. Usually, people don't consciously decide to sin; they just drift into it by rationalizing or ignoring the stop signs they should have noticed. Institutions can do the same, and ambition can worm its way insidiously into the best intentions. With all due respect to Sorin's first rector, Father Morrissey's prophecy was hilariously off base. Today we are among the richest private institutions in the country, and the debate swirls about whether we are sacrificing too much of our Catholic character in order to keep pace with the academic Joneses who are our neighbors atop the higher education mountain.

There is a standing order to have a crucifix in every classroom. We do have a smattering of faculty priests, sisters, and brothers, along with a good number more in staff positions. We hold more conferences on religion than just about anywhere else and sponsor a handful of programs rooted in Catholic social teaching, but it is also true that much of our classroom instruction resembles the offerings to be found elsewhere in American academe.

There is a sizeable yet shrinking number of lay faculty here who remain devoted to the belief that faith should inform one's intellectual development, and we have adopted hiring targets for maintaining a majority share of Catholic scholars. However, those totals have been declining steadily despite a dramatic warning in a strategic plan from twenty-five years ago that Notre Dame would cease to maintain its Catholic character within a generation or two were that trend not reversed.

It is not inevitable that the University will succeed in this century in its attempts to balance the complementary relationship between faith and reason, or as Father Moreau would put it, the life of the heart and mind. Notre Dame could drift beyond the tipping point, like most other universities founded with a religious affiliation have. Still, there are so many times when this institution appeared to be lost yet emerged even stronger from its travails, I cannot help but believe that God has a few more unexpected favors to bestow upon us. And, since our campus leadership appears quite earnest about recruiting more Catholics and others who embrace its religious tradition, I'm gambling that we still have one generation left.

Perhaps this account will provide some insight for those who have had no personal connection with us, though frankly, my main hope is that this story will sharpen the appreciation of those who have. It is sometimes a place which some well-meaning people term "magical," yet that is as inadequate a description as cynical references to Our Lady's University as a "football factory."

Notre Dame did not drop out of the sky, and the close bonds its graduates feel to the place were nurtured from the moment Father Sorin started stocking library books written in English. Little about this place is accidental. At the turn of the twentieth century, Holy Cross priests were the ones pressing for acceptance into the Big Ten, as Murray Sperber points out in his book, Shake Down the Thunder. Notre Dame was fortunate that a Norwegian Protestant dropped in and accelerated the legend-making, but football glory was part of a bold clerical marketing plan brewing years before Rockne ever drew an X or O on an athletic department blackboard.

Nearly a hundred years later, Father Jenkins challenged the Notre Dame community in his 2005 inaugural speech with these words: "If we are afraid to be different from the world, how can we make a difference IN the world?" We need to hold one another to that standard. Jesus Christ taught us that in order to save our lives we must lose them. The reason why I like the Potter books, particularly the last, is that their message is similar. I am glad that they have given this generation a few more tools and incentives to become heroes, especially for those reluctant to take the word of their rectors on faith.

It is good to be a great institution, but Christ only mentions the term "greatness" within the context of His disciples' need to be humble. On the other hand, He also called them to be perfect. Our ability to avoid straying across the fuzzy line that separates questing for excellence from grasping for prestige depends upon us remaining institutionally self-confident enough to determine our own standards within the context of the Gospel.

The University tends to get pilloried publicly at both ends of the media spectrum. On one hand, we are accused of aping corporate America by signing exclusive football contracts with NBC, but we also catch grief for maintaining higher academic standards for student-athletes even when it hurts our recruiting efforts. There is an ugliness to indiscriminate charges of hypocrisy because we make the effort to achieve some reasonable balance, but maybe being whipsawed in the middle is the right place to be stuck. It hurts sometimes, but it's a good way to be kept honest.

There are indeed grounds for criticism because it is a delicate juggling act, and we who live here are not incapable of objectively searching our souls at times about the institutional playbook. Notre Dame has evolved and expanded exponentially since the horse and buggy days of J.E. Cusack. It has unquestionably become more corporate and bureaucratic and its internal power struggles at times uncomfortably public. It certainly aspires to be a bigger player in the Church and in civil society. It's also true that we have difficulty at times getting all of our various constituents on board with the notion, if pushed to the wall, that our mission matters more than our academic or athletic rankings.

John Wooden, the legendary former UCLA basketball coach, once made an important distinction: "Be more concerned with your character than your reputation because your character is what you really are, while your reputation is merely what others think you are." After ten NCAA basketball titles, his example demonstrates the ironic truth that the best way to be number one is for individuals and institutions to remain faithful to their own creed rather than adopting winning as an end in itself. It's the long way to the top, but as I tell my students frequently, "The hard road is usually the right one."

The University encapsulates the difficulties Catholics face in many different arenas, trying to uphold their faith while aspiring to preeminence among its secular peers. The right mix is elusive, and the stakes high. Were the brazen, charming, visionary, and bull-headed founder, Father Sorin, to return today reincarnated as a twenty-first century clerical executive, he would doubtless be frustrated at how much more difficult it is to make this thoroughly modern institution obedient to one person's vision. I'm not sure whether I would want him to be president in this age or not. It depends upon the day and the issue.

However, whatever its flaws, I prefer to look at this place through the prism of periodic conversations I catch between students from other schools who road trip here and the residents they have come to visit. To outsiders the system seems alien or just plain weird. I am invariably amused by their puzzled looks when they hear there are no coed dorms and wonder that anyone would bother to enforce a concept as retrograde as parietal hours in this modern age. Then I listen to Sorin Otters respond by bragging about their residence hall's unique traditions, explaining why they touch Father Sorin's toe each time they pass his statue by the front door, and telling stories about the rector who lives down the corridor – sometimes sticking up for us with stalwart defenses like, "He's OK for a priest."

Our work in residence halls is the Holy Cross "family business" more than any other part of our ministry at Notre Dame. We monopolized it entirely for most of the University's history, and many of the priests and brothers who have gone before us struggled mightily to balance full academic or administrative loads with supervising scores of high-octane undergraduates. That dual role has become nearly impossible to maintain in an age of specialization, but most of those teaching and researching continue to share hallways with students as in-residence priests, some into their seventies, even if they are not the ones patrolling hallways until 3:00 AM. It is no accident that today that we retain a larger share of positions in residence life than any other, despite many demands upon our personnel.

I have learned so much sitting at night listening to the stories of mentors and elders who have preceded me that I am hard pressed to imagine how I could otherwise persevere in this role without that support. I constantly find relief in the knowledge that others have survived their challenges for generations before me and laugh readily about their battle scars. I am blessed to have had the benefit of learning at the Holy Cross family table how to take irritating behaviors in stride and – mostly – resist the temptation to inflame them into conflagrations. There is a font of wisdom in Corby Hall among the C.S.C.'s who gather there that people like me draw upon and absorb indirectly through osmosis over the years and is greater than any combination of orientation sessions and workshops I will ever attend. Those plug the gaps, but there is no substitute for living with people who have spent decades lumbering around the corridors of our residence halls.

The feeling I have whenever I walk over to Corby for prayer, meals, or relaxation with other Holy Cross religious is not much different than the atmosphere in our dorms. It is admittedly tamer, and sobriety is usually easier to enforce! But our community life is also infused with the same sense of family that our students leave here treasuring. Sometimes we disseminate it simply through sharing walls and absorbing the same air. Other times, our form of instruction is more pointed and intentional. I am confident that Father Moreau would approve of us employing a variety of methods for the ends he envisioned.

It might seem anachronistic to the outside observer for every hall to have its own chapel and Sunday night Mass, but a number of those are standing room only. Their existence in each one is hardly a random design quirk. We deliberately make it easy for our students to get to church and experience Christ in the midst of whatever other chaos may be enveloping their surroundings. The chapels and our own presence in those halls is a package deal. Some attribute the number of students living on campus to the low-grade quality of off-campus housing or the historical centrality of residence halls in the campus' social structure. However, the latter begs the question of how the life within them came to matter so much in the first place.

We have tried by living among our students to instruct them in manners, social skills, tact, discretion, self-discipline, commitment, leadership, and integrity. We encourage our charges to study what they love and embrace the opportunity to expand their intellects. I think every rector attempts to promote virtues like: generosity, compassion, the importance of cultivating a forgiving spirit, service to one's neighbor, and a persistent dedication to exploring the truths that lie deeply within one's soul. We should always welcome the occasional theological question from a persistent sophomore searching for deeper answers, even while parrying their jokes. We need to share our own faith openly by the way we comfort sinners and preach the Word so that it spreads beyond these walls. It helps to maintain a good sense of humor in the face of their more innocent escapades, and it is healthy sometimes to let them see our own warts beneath the piles of press clippings.

Students might not always applaud our management styles when their choices don't leave us in a laughing mood, but is important to be close at hand when they need to be reminded of their responsibility to grow into adults – or when a personal crisis strikes and makes them grow up even quicker. If we sometimes give them more breaks than they deserve, maybe the whole point is that we believe their essential goodness will win over all, whatever the odds. Institutionally, Notre Dame leans more toward Aquinas' confidence in grace building upon nature than Augustine's preoccupation with sin. We do witness plenty of sinfulness in our students but even more evidence that Aquinas' was right about human beings' natural inclinations. Most of them turn out pretty well in the end and some a lot better.

If I ever left this patch of ground for someplace like northern Uganda where children have been forced to kill their playmates as an indoctrination exercise into a madman's army, my theological framework would likely acquire a darker tinge. We are a protective cocoon here, but the troubles of our times suggest that we should be fashioning more, rather than fewer, havens where tomorrow heroes can nourish their ideals.

*   *   *

It is reassuring to know that Notre Dame graduates are distinguished by their gratitude and loyalty to their alma mater. Just as they attend church more than others in their age group, so too do they send a far greater percentage of sons and daughters here than do alumni of any other American college or university. Stanford and Yale at nine percent each lag far behind our student body composed of nearly one-fourth alumni children, and Notre Dame follows only Princeton by one or two points in its rate of contributing alumni.

The University also dispatches a disproportionate number of women and men to convents and seminaries other than our own, if in lower absolute numbers than the halcyon days of the 1950s. It is not unusual for a diocese to have more ND grads in its seminary than from any other Catholic college or university. It's hard not to conclude from those statistics that most of our constituents are fairly satisfied customers who come to appreciate that the distinctiveness of Notre Dame's mission will mark them wherever they go. Ours are usually proud and rarely indifferent about their years spent under our roofs. They tend to grow more grateful for what we have wrought here as the years unfold, and they start to deal with kids bouncing off the walls of their own homes.

Few hold ambiguous opinions about the University dedicated to the Mother of God, whatever parts of the University fall under the scrutiny of their spotlights. It has always marched to its own rhythm, somewhat distinct even from the Church which claims its primary loyalty – one dictated from the outset by an unusual combination of religious devotion, family atmosphere, commitment to teaching, appreciation for scholarship, and a fiercely competitive spirit that permeates it bricks and cannot be found anywhere else. The longer I stay, the more I agree with Father Hesburgh that a woman named Mary deserves most of the credit, though I'll give the second and third spots to Fathers Sorin and Moreau. After thirty years, it's the only thing that makes any sense to me.

These influences do not always mesh well together, and even those who profess to love this place sometimes grow exasperated with its contradictions as we who live with our students sometimes get frustrated with theirs. I hope that this book will enhance the understanding of the critical role that our philosophy of residentiality plays in the lives of our students, whether they have resided in Sorin College or in one of its lesser imitators.

*   *   *

Twenty years ago, I was sitting in a theology class listening to a professor ridicule the Father O'Malley model of priesthood. It was patriarchal and hopelessly outdated, he asserted. I went back and watched *Going My Way*. I was surprised by what I found. He was hip enough to understand and relate well to young people but didn't try to be their best buddy. He was equally comfortable wearing gym clothes or a collar. He was patient with lesser evils and watchful without prying more than necessary. He could cite theology texts but normally tried to persuade with common sense rather than assaulting parishioners or their children with doctrinal firepower.

At one point in the sixty-plus-year-old movie, Father O'Malley tries to help a young woman who had gotten into trouble, giving her money out his pocket that he had no rational reason for believing would ever be repaid. He realized it was more important to be a lifeline than judge her mistake. He usually said less than he knew and was able to kid around yet pull his charges up short when needed, subtly nudging them all the while to become an-gelic-sounding choir boys despite their initial resistance. He un-derstood that it was important for both their voices and hearts to sing. I suppose I am a throwback who came of age in an Irish ghetto that still embraced the schmaltzy Hollywood Catholicism of a long-vanished era, but I believe that good chunks of that model are eminently salvageable and even needed.

Perhaps decades from now observers will look back and conclude with hindsight that Notre Dame was on the verge of becoming a dinosaur as my words were being logged onto a computer screen. However, I am convinced that the model for student life envisioned by Fathers Moreau and Sorin is time-less. Minds and hearts need equal attention, and caring for them individually never goes out of style, though the mission will be packaged differently depending upon whether the age prizes a laptop or a horse more.

I have heard Father Ted claim that the rector's job is the best on campus because we have the most quality contact with our students. He's right about most things, and I think he's spot on about that. He has also said that if he could choose one word for his tombstone, it would be "Priest." I like that too, although I might not mind if someone added "and Rector" to mine. We'll see how long I last.

CHAPTER 18

A Gift for Molly

I HAVE BEEN A HOLY CROSS PRIEST for almost twenty years, three-quarters of that at Notre Dame. Staying up until two or three or four in the morning when there isn't anything but paid programming left on cable fits like a shabby old moccasin now. If I had spent the last two decades getting up for the parish's 7:00 AM Mass, I doubt that I could jumpstart myself into this life now as fifty looms on the horizon.

While the setting seems strange to priests elsewhere, I think it helps to keep us from becoming odd. It's hard for a celibate male to grow too eccentric and remain halfway relevant when his main preoccupation is the same as other people his age: a boisterous horde of kids breezily dumping smelly hockey pads and dirty laundry in the hallways. Well, that's the boys anyway.

I know that my life path has been altered for the better by those like Father George who tolerated our foolishness in the distant '70s. They had the good sense to let us figure out some of it for ourselves and nail us to the wall at other times. Now

I appreciate better how many restless nights we caused our parents before we arrived here and later our rectors once we hit the Main Circle in overloaded gas guzzlers.

I expect my crazy life to continue much as it has been. It is a little schizophrenic and certainly paradoxical. I enjoy weekdays when nothing more serious than Dollar Derby is going on outside my door much more than weekends stepping over spots of vomoose spread over vomit on the carpet. Most of all, I relish standing behind the altar looking out at them during Sunday Mass, even if I do groan through the post-communion announcements. From that vantage point they look more like angels than demons, though I never quite know which incarnation I will encounter turning a hallway corner on a Friday night.

Sometimes I hit the wall and begin asking myself why I'm here at all when there are a couple of thousand priestless parishes scattered throughout the country. I suppose it all comes down to the realization that these students are the most promising prospects for our future, rambunctious but talented and intuitively generous conveyors of grace to the Church and world. As long as some of us can tolerate their follies and keep vampire hours without chomping their heads off in frustration, some few of us should spend this critical time with them.

Perhaps what we do here at Notre Dame isn't normal in the context of today's American college culture, but it is fairly standard to be a middle-aged man, infuriated with an eighteen or nineteen year old one minute and extremely proud of him the next. I do at times become frustrated, exasperated, exhausted, and even appalled by their waywardness. I grow more patient whenever I hearken back to the era of tube socks and bell bottoms, when I was a nervous, naïve, and reckless city kid who beamed down the Indiana Toll Road from Chicago. I'm not their dad, but I am pleased to share wall and ceiling space with them as their "Father" for a few short years.

*   *   *

I sometimes think the Amish and Mormons have it figured out better than Catholics. The Amish let their kids go "wilding" in their late teens, two years to get their cravings out of their systems before freely making a decision as to whether or not they want to commit to adult life in the community. The Mormons require college-agers to go on service mission for two years, usually to a foreign country. We are rightly proud that a larger proportion of ours participate in overseas study programs than any other American university, but I don't think it would be such a bad idea if we required all of them to do a year of service or study abroad learning how to communicate in another language in order to acquire a Notre Dame degree.

It's fairly normal for European students to have a "gap year," and there is some evidence a higher percentage of those in our country who give it a shot graduate from college than those who don't. I have encouraged a few graduating seniors who were confused about what to do next to buy a one-way, trans-Atlantic ticket and a backpack, then spend six to twelve months learning how to fend for themselves. It's also good out-of-the-classroom education for a privileged young person to experience what it's

253

like to be an illegal immigrant scrambling for a dishwashing job in order to eat.

The objection, of course, is that everyone doesn't need to spend a whole year speaking French or Mandarin to become a mature adult. However, they certainly acquire valuable survival skills when they are stranded in a Hungarian train station at 3:00 AM and they absorb more culture even when sleepwalking through Baroque churches, Renaissance palaces, and cobblestone throughways than they would eating at Outback or shopping at Nordstrom's. Others might realize in their explorations of other cultures that there are more options – and more to a vocation – than majoring in business solely to make a buck.

We have always expected our students to manage a lot in the time between their doe-eyed arrival and the lingering, poignant days of Senior Week: move away from home; succeed in a high powered academic environment; discern their life path with little real world experience; mature emotionally; handle being cast adrift to revel in their "freedom;" and begin to forge their identity as adults. But in my South Side high school, gang members stashed knives in lockers while today angry teenagers pile up machine guns in garages. At times, my life felt like *West Side Story,* but it was an idyllic existence compared to Columbine High.

In the Animal House era, teenage suicide wasn't an epidemic; ADD was an elementary school math term; and there were only a handful taking allergy or asthma medication, let alone Prozac or Zoloft. Their DNA codes couldn't have changed that much in thirty years, but their culture, schools, and homes certainly have. We may have tipped a few too many Solo cups in the

'70s, but not many of us were so sick either. If we were taking drugs, it was mostly because we wanted to, not because we had to. Then again, maybe we've passed on more of ourselves than we intended and have more penance to do.

An eighteen or nineteen year old doesn't grow up by chatting with Mom or Dad three times a day on the cell phone and telling them *everything,* but bingeing at off-campus keg parties on weekends like frat boys (or sorority girls) doesn't raise their maturity level either. There is an elusive balance somewhere in there – between knowing what they're up to and letting them figure it out for themselves, keeping a close eye on them and handing them plane tickets to wander the continents.

At the end of the day, whether through grace or chance, counseling or prayer, an attentive RA or the support of friends, few roll into a ditch, literally or figuratively, but some do hug the security of an educational cocoon and graduate as seniors uncertain about how to navigate their way beyond it. It's just a suggestion that they spend some time away as a degree requirement, and since it would probably reduce our applicant pool significantly, I don't expect it to be taken seriously. On the other hand, I also have to admit that there are others for whom just a few short weeks abroad is enough to transform their lives and cause ripples of grace in many others.

*   *   *

The first chapter related a story about Michael who raised enough money to build a dormitory in Uganda, sweated out a bad case of malaria, and now dreams of eradicating poverty-rooted diseases throughout Africa. The last is coming to an end with a story about a fifteen-year-old girl named Molly who is growing up just outside of Denver.

Pat, who went to Uganda the following summer and raised more than three times as much money, returned to campus several months later after a semester in London. He didn't get his name on a building, though some of the funds he raised went toward a boys' residence already in progress, a fence, a kitchen, and, amusingly enough, a block of rather primitive pit toilets. So, when I visited Uganda and St. Jude's for the first time in July 2007, I printed a sign in magic marker with the words, "Pat's Privy," stuck it over one of the waste holes in the floor, took a photo, and had it framed and waiting for him when he showed up for his senior year. I just couldn't pass up the opportunity to have a little fun with an incoming RA who appreciated the importance of infrastructure.

After his summer at St. Jude's, Pat only had a couple of weeks at home before leaving for London. Somehow in that short time, he managed to put together the fifty- piece slide show that formed the core of his fundraising campaign for the school. He returned home four months later in time for Christmas and his twenty-first birthday on December 26.

That post-Christmas morning his parents told him that they were saving his birthday presents for later – except for his sister Molly's. She just couldn't wait and handed him an envelope. In it was $250, her life savings except for $20 she held back, her contribution to Pat's St. Jude fundraising campaign. When he asked how she was going to buy things for herself, she said, "I can't think of anything else I need." Like the widow in the gospel who deposits her few coins in the collection box, Molly gave just about all she had because others needed it more.

After hearing that story from her proud older brother, I initially planned to send her a gift, maybe a book on Uganda or some piece of native craft art. Instead, I decided to wait and make this ending my gift to her on behalf of those kids – and me. I just hope Molly's parents don't mind the foretaste of college party life it took to reach it. It was a risk to wait to express my gratitude, like I said in the first chapter, that I would ever finish what I knew I should do. While Michael's work inspired the first words written in my journal, Pat's little sister motivated me to sprint ahead to the finish when I was stalled and needed a boost.

Molly, you're getting the first copy still warm off the presses. Thank you for a gift that truly was of biblical proportions. Your example teaches those of us who are educators with lots of credentials and letters after our names that generosity is a greater blessing than status, success, prestige, or even native intelligence. Yours was not a gift of the mind but one from the depth of your heart. That is the place where we all can find God if we have the courage to burrow there persistently deep beneath the flotsam of our daily foibles. It is one of the more important lessons that Notre Dame students should and often do learn during their years within our walls, just as Fathers Moreau and Sorin foresaw more than a century and a half ago when Notre Dame was merely the name of a big cathedral in Paris.

And, by the way, thank you too, Mike and Jean. If I'm right that the fruit doesn't land far from the tree, then your kids sprang from a couple of redwoods.

*   *   *

Despite Notre Dame's institutional growth challenges, persistent troubles with alcohol induced stupidity, temptations to toss off clothes, and sheer daily wackiness, I am privileged to be at a place that has a philosophy grounded in the elusive pursuit of virtue. As Father Jenkins put it in a homily in January 2007 on the feast of St. Thomas Aquinas, "While we seek the truth, we also seek to be holy." That high bar leaves us with plenty of space for disappointment, but it also gives our students something noble to measure themselves by and pray over.

Some critics think that in *loco parentis* is outdated. We've downplayed the use of the term since the '70s, but the mental, physical, academic, personal, and spiritual well-being of our students demands that someone toss those speed bumps in their paths and stay up praying they make it home at night. We can't make their choices for them, but we can try to raise their sights both in and out of the classroom.

A couple of years ago, I received a letter from a college friend who is a physician. He is content with his career, marriage, and children and considers himself blessed. Nevertheless, he regretted that he did not have more time to donate to those who lack access to the world's best medicine. I realized that his thoughts attest quite accurately to what a Notre Dame education should be and still remains at its best — a constant itch scratching our consciences long after the Dome has disappeared in the rear view mirror, compelling our graduates to ponder how they can spend the time they have doing more for those who have less.

*   *   *

I have lived in two places that taught me wildly different lessons. The neighborhood of my childhood led me to believe that most things were black and white, Catholic or non-Catholic, Democrat or Republican, pro-union or pro-management, Sox or Cubs, for us or against. Perhaps that is why it now feels like alien territory to which I return infrequently, except when I need a refresher course in loyalty or feel like taking in a ballgame. However, I also acknowledge that my family and neighbors' blue-collar outlook made me a pragmatist with a short fuse for pretence. Those qualities have generally served me well, especially in dwelling among late adolescent barbarians! I'm less sure about the virtue of their other legacy, the gift for sarcasm that my staff skewered me for in their heartfelt letter.

There were a lot of South Side Chicago Irish punks like me there in a world that has been fading since I was born. When I first went to Ireland twelve years ago, I began to understand why my grandfather and others like him cut themselves off emotionally and rarely spoke about it to their children. My great-grandparents raised thirteen children to adulthood in a three-room cottage with an open hearth for cooking and an outhouse next to a turf bog. Those who emigrated had indoor plumbing here, but the first generation didn't do that much better working in Chicago cattle pens in place of rock-strewn Clare pastures. There was nothing to go back to, but they hadn't yet achieved much worth bragging about to those they left behind. One grandfather worked in a cold storage warehouse, and my second-generation father loaded trucks most of his life like his father-in-law. They bought lace curtains for special occasions but never made it to Beverly with the politicians or to the North Shore with the bankers. They harbored few dreams for themselves but many for their kids. It is no surprise that they looked upon Notre Dame as subway alumni heaven.

But by the time I arrived here in 1977, few of my classmates from the burbs had any idea what it was like to walk less than a block each Sunday to the neighborhood church built with immigrant nickels and dimes. I am, however, pleased that thirty years later our students still do know what it is like to stroll each Sunday down the halls of their dorms for Mass and pack a chapel at a not-so-godly hour. I hope that is the one thing about this place that never changes, or this will not be Notre Dame.

Despite several detours that might have led me away, Notre Dame has firmly supplanted my birthplace as the home to which I keep returning. At times, living here doesn't feel so much different from a few weeks of giddy chaos of White Sox Boys' Camp, yet at other moments I am fortunate to see previews of future adult accomplishments and glimmers of holiness in some who yearn for more than clichéd definitions of success.

Like a lot of others, the honey in the trap pulling me here originated with football fanaticism more than religion or academic excellence, but it is frequently true that we find our deeper calling from what some label serendipity but others know as grace. I heard the strains of alleluias in my hallway one night and came to discover my vocation, but mine is not the only life that has been irrevocably shaped by the ongoing strains of faith in the midst of late adolescent chaos.

*   *   *

The summer before this book made its way into print, Ken Woodward from *Newsweek,* who graduated from here fifty years ago, wrote in an article for *Notre Dame Magazine* that "the University looks best to me from some point midway between close up, where ordinary blemishes show, and far away where her distinctive beauty blurs." I know what he means, but I have purposefully leaned more toward our blackheads and ingrown hairs in these pages than the coffee table books that display the splendor of Notre Dame's lakes, trees, and mountains of bricks in Technicolor hues.

It is as necessary to treasure our grittiness as to gaze in awe at the Basilica and Dome on a sapphire-blue summer day if we really want to keep the big picture about what transpires within our boundaries before us. A Miss America's face would appear ugly under a microscope at first glance too, but it is just a different perspective that allows us to appreciate our humanity more. After all these years of looking at this place from many angles, I find it difficult to be objective. Still, as I navigate warily around the moldy corridors of Sorin College subjecting Notre Dame to the microscope test, I appreciate how our students' stumblings, often more than their successes, frequently beget life-changing transformations, though the resulting yarns are nowhere near so romantic as our myths.

Just as the resurrection would be senseless without the cross, so too does growth into adulthood inevitably entail some transformation out of reckless behavior and childish naiveté. The motto of the Congregation of Holy Cross is, "The cross, our only hope." On the surface, it seems foolish to stand hopeful in the face of the ultimate tragedy. However, the real foolishness is that human beings put to death the one who best embodied every one of our deepest hopes. The mystery of the cross is that God's forgiveness and joy in us persist anyway. Our hope, ultimately our only true hope, is the knowledge that He gives us multiple opportunities to discover the goodness within and be redeemed even when we don't merit a sliver of it.

I have learned through living side by side with our students that life is filled with subtle ironies. All human beings are paradoxes riddled with inconsistencies, much like this manuscript which careens between delight and frustration with the echoes of drum sets and plastic horns lingering in the air around me. I expect to be surprised now that I understand people are not so predictable, and I am grateful that people like me always have more to learn from those we teach. My Holy Cross brothers occasionally remind me that I harbor many opinions, but I am compelled to confess that there are few things of which I am certain. However, I do know that, thirty years after leaving Chicago, a simple concrete cross in the cemetery along St. Mary's Road at Notre Dame will mark my final destination, even though I never dreamed of making a permanent home in Indiana.

I believe more than ever in the profound truth written on the final page of Georges Bernanos' *The Diary of a Country Priest:* "Does it matter? Grace is everywhere." Those are the last words uttered by the novel's dying young curate to a layman friend taken aback when asked to provide forgiveness in the absence of a clerical confessor. We have many layers to our lives and must probe deeply for it sometimes. Nevertheless, the antics and potholes, laughter and guy tears, and sometimes even the tragedies marking the trails of Otters, Dawgs, Phoxes, and other students mask an abundance of grace within. Over the course of these thirty years, I have become convinced that serendipity is grossly overrated and exerts little power outside of a casino. Instead, I find goodness repeatedly triumphing over disappointment and gratitude trumping resentment.

I have accumulated a fair number of important lessons and entertaining tales since I first arrived here, but there are thousands more to tell by others who have left their names in the bricks of this overachieving Catholic Hoosierville dedicated to the Mother of God. We often speak casually of "The" Notre Dame Experience, but the roads that lead away from here are as varied as the ones that bring each of us to the Main Gate for the first time as seventeen- or eighteen-year-old newbies. My collection of stories is simply part of the path I have been led to travel and constitute a longer version of what I say to parents each August of why most days, if not every weekend night, I am blessed to be a stay-at-home priest at Notre Dame.

ABOUT THE AUTHOR

FR. JIM KING, C.S.C. is in his fifth year as rector of Sorin College. He served as Director of Vocations for the Congregation of Holy Cross, Indiana Province from 1997-2005. For five years previous to that, he was assigned to the University of Portland as a residence hall director, alumni and development staffer, and overseas director of its Salzburg Program. He has also taught as an instructor at both universities. He graduated from the University of Notre Dame in 1981, was ordained a Holy Cross priest in 1988, received a master's degree in political science from the University of Wisconsin in 1992, and completed a master's degree in nonprofit administration in 2007. Fr. King is originally from Chicago.